W9-AAE-441

Also by Michael Robbins

Alien vs. Predator
The Second Sex

EQUIPMENT FOR LIVING

On Poetry

and

Pop Music

* * *

Michael Robbins

Simon & Schuster

New York   London   Toronto   Sydney   New Delhi

Simon & Schuster
1230 Avenue of the Americas
New York, NY 10020

First Simon & Schuster hardcover edition July 2017

SIMON & SCHUSTER and colophon are registered
trademarks of Simon & Schuster, Inc.

For information about special discounts for bulk purchases,
please contact Simon & Schuster Special Sales at 1-866-506-1949
or business@simonandschuster.com.

The Simon & Schuster Speakers Bureau can bring authors to
your live event. For more information or to book an event contact
the Simon & Schuster Speakers Bureau at 1-866-248-3049 or
visit our website at www.simonspeakers.com.

Interior design by Lewelin Polanco

Manufactured in the United States of America

1 3 5 7 9 10 8 6 4 2

Library of Congress Cataloging-in-Publication Data is available.

ISBN 978-1-4767-4709-5
ISBN 978-1-4767-4711-8 (ebook)

For my dad, who let me play his records,
and in memory of Prince Rogers Nelson

CONTENTS

I know my lazy, leaden twang
Is like the reason in a storm;

And yet it brings the storm to bear.
I twang it out and leave it there.

—WALLACE STEVENS

"

EQUIPMENT FOR LIVING

"A new thing appears," Annie Dillard writes, "as if we needed a new thing."[1] What are we *doing* with all these films and songs and novels and poems and pictures? Why keep making them? Don't we have enough, or too much?

I find I can't get away from my early reading of Harold Bloom, who proposes that we ask of a text: "What is it good for, what can I do with it, what can it do for me, what can I make it mean?"[2] Things that answer these questions—things that are good for something, that we can do something with, that we can make do things for us, that we can make mean something—we might call equipment.

Hammers, for instance, are good for lots of things—building birdhouses, bludgeoning ideological opponents, breaking down and becoming present-at-hand. But a hammer is obviously designed in such a way that certain purposes (driving nails) are more plausible than others. For Kenneth Burke, poetry is designed for *living*: "Poetry *is* produced . . . as part of the *consolatio philosophiae*. It is undertaken as *equipment for living*, as a ritualistic way of arming us to confront perplexities and risks. It would *protect* us."[3]

I like the notion that the aesthetic is conceived in response to threat. Burke reminds us that implicit in the notion of protection is the idea of something to be *protected against*. Risks and perplexities. The shit that, in the vernacular version, happens.

What Burke does *not* mean by *equipment for living* is conveyed by Kenneth Koch's line: "People say yes everyone is dying / But here read this happy book on the subject." Poetry doesn't kiss the boo-boo and make it all better. Burke suggests that poems be viewed as "strategies for dealing with situations" (he doesn't say this is the only way to view them). The structural defects of our existence require of us strategic thinking. Burke consults some dictionaries and discovers that *strategy* has to do with the movement and directing of armies:

> Surely the most highly alembicated and sophisticated work of art, arising in complex civilizations, could be considered as designed to organize and command the army of one's thoughts and images, and to so organize them that one "imposes upon the enemy the time and place and conditions for fighting preferred by oneself." One seeks to "direct the larger movements and operations" in one's campaign of living.[4]

Burke rejects the "strategy for easy consolation" found in "popular 'inspirational literature,' " art as uplift, paper armies raised on the cheap. "All the redemption I can offer," Bruce Springsteen admits, "is beneath this dirty hood." In *The Triumph of Love*, Geoffrey Hill asks, "What are poems for?" His answer, borrowed from Giacomo Leopardi, is not without its self-directed irony:

> They are to console us
> with their own gift, which is like perfect pitch.
> Let us commit that to our dust. What
> ought a poem to be? Answer, *a sad*
> *and angry consolation.* What is
> the poem? What figures? Say,
> *a sad and angry consolation.* That's
> beautiful. Once more? *A sad and angry*
> *consolation.*

The repetition of Leopardi's phrase forms a call-and-response, with the emphasis shifting as each adjective ends a line in turn. But as if to underscore the unromantic tenor of Hill's vision, the exchange is hardly "Can I get an amen?" No one's likely to get fired up over "Once more? *A sad and angry consolation.*"

But the words return, a refrain, as a trauma is repeated in Freud's *Beyond the Pleasure Principle*, and we are to commit them to the dust unto which, Genesis tells us, we shall return (the dirty hood of the grave). The mantra-like repetition of *a sad and angry consolation* makes the words seem less clear, more in need of interpretation. The question that forces itself is, of course, how something consoling can be sad and angry, or how sorrow and anger can console, when these would seem to be precisely the conditions for which sufferers need consolation.

Boethius would have understood: he composed *De Consolatione Philosophiae* in prison, awaiting execution. According to one reputable source, "a cord was twisted round his head so tightly that it caused his eyeballs to protrude from their sockets, and . . . his life was then beaten out of him by a club."[5] Lady Philosophy does not console the prisoner by freeing him or providing him with worldly goods or happiness, but by reconciling him to his fate. He comes to accept that all things are ordered sweetly by God, and he aspires to achieve spiritual freedom through contemplation of God. (Actual redemption is implied, but not easy consolation.)

Nietzsche saw art, and Lady Philosophy, as a benign illusion that sustains us in the face of the awful truth, which would cause our eyeballs to protrude from their sockets. My understanding of poetry's consolatory powers has more in common with psychoanalysis as a way of fortifying the self through the acceptance of perpetual unrest. Our wills and fates do so contrary run that not even our wills are under our control. I wouldn't be the first to see psychoanalysis in this sense as a trope for poetry (or vice versa). In Adam Phillips's psychoanalytical version of Bloom's pragmatism, a text answers the question "what can it get you out of?"[6] One thing it can get you out of is the false hope that you can escape unrest.

"No one here gets out alive" is the *best-case scenario*. Consolation is not false comfort. Poetry's a prophylactic, not a vaccine. One way poetry helps you to accept perpetual unrest, to arm yourself to confront perplexities, is by reminding you that you're not alone (a not coincidentally common refrain in popular song). This just in: Everyone you love will be extinguished, and so will you. You're not special. Men and women have been living and dying for a long time, and some of them have left records. Those records won't eliminate your fears; they might help you to live with them. They might help you raise an army.

It isn't only at the level of subject (what's often miscalled "content") that poetry operates as equipment for living. "Every atom belonging to me as good belongs to you" teaches us that we are involved in humankind, but so does "Oh, look what you've done to this rock 'n' roll clow-ow-own." Yes, I assume that what Burke says about poetry applies, mutatis mutandis, to the songs of Def Leppard, though they are hardly alembicated at all.* My justification for this assumption is formal. Both poems and pop songs provide what Burke calls "structural assertion": "Form, a public matter that symbolically enrolls us with allies who will share the burdens with us."[7]

Which means what, exactly? *Form* is notoriously hard to define. *The Princeton Encyclopedia of Poetry & Poetics*: "The *OED* gives 22 definitions, with subcategory refinements and variations."[8] The traditional distinction between *form* and *content* doesn't hold for a variety of reasons. Form shapes meaning, so meaning shifts when form does—in Peter McDonald's phrase, form "is the pressing reality according to which metaphors and meaning must make their way."[9] The relationship of form and content is more like that

---

* R. P. Blackmur: "I think on the whole [Burke's] method could be applied with equal fruitfulness to Shakespeare, Dashiell Hammett, or Marie Corelli." Burke: "When I got through wincing, I had to admit that Blackmur was right. . . . You can't properly put Marie Corelli and Shakespeare apart until you have first put them together" (Quoted in Burke, 302).

of space and time than that of vessel and water. For my purposes, *form* means something like: those features that make a given verbal act shareable. As Burke notes, "Language, of all things, is most public, most collective, in its substance."[10] There's no such thing as a private language; language is a social fact. So, because of its conditions of production and consumption, is pop music. A pop song is a *popular* song, one that some ideal "everybody" knows or could know. Its form lends itself to communal participation. Or, stronger, it depends upon the possibility of communal participation for its full effect. Burke's "structural assertion" is a neat way of recognizing that form is involved in any artifact—the tax code, for instance—but that the structure of some artifacts (poems, pop songs) asserts itself more strongly, stakes its claim on our attention more enticingly, and thereby possesses a greater degree of shareability.

Form grounds us in a community, however attenuated or virtual. My friend Jen writes that, on a summer night in Brooklyn outside a club, "Rose and I were singing 'We Can't Stop' to each other. She would sing the *la da dee da dee* parts and I would sing *This is our house, this is our rules*. It's a beautiful song." Jen and Rose are already allies, but, sharing some words and a melody (Miley Cyrus's, in this case), they take their place symbolically among others who know the song, who sing along. A passerby might join in for a few bars, exchanging smiles with these strangers who are linked to him, however briefly, through the public matter of form: an occasion for artifactual embrace. It's magic (just a little bit of magic).

This is why the bus scene in Cameron Crowe's otherwise risible movie *Almost Famous* is so powerful. Everyone on the tour bus—the band, the groupies, the critic—is pissed off at everybody else for various reasons. Everyone's got that stuck-in-a-confined-space-with-people-I-want-to-kill stare. Elton John's "Tiny Dancer" comes on the stereo, and for a while the band members continue to glower, but finally the bassist starts singing along: "Handing tickets out for *Gah*-awd." Kate Hudson joins in on the next line, and most of the bus is smiling and singing by the time Elton gets to "The boulevard is not that bad." It's corny, but it's true: everyone knows the lines by heart, everyone throws their head back and closes their eyes and belts out the chorus. It works, I want to say, for the same reason the Kaddish or the Mass works: it conveys comfort because it is a shared experience, one that reinforces a sense of community, of "allies who will share the burdens with us." The entire congregation's voices are lifted in unison, in supplication, in awe—the form is universal, known to all.

One church might be distinguished from others by its forms. The televangelical *JAY*-zus, the sober Jesu Christe of the Latin Mass, the radical Jewish peasant Yeshua of Nazareth of Guy Davenport's translations, and the *Gee-zuhhs* of Norman Greenbaum's "gotta have a friend in" are not the same sort of equipment. The difference between the Eucharist and "Tiny Dancer" is the difference between *God* and *Gah-awd*, between an abstract principle of general transcendence and a practical occasion for transcendence as a shareable idiosyncrasy. It is *Gah-awd* (rather than *God*) that recruits community into the world specified by the "content"—in which the boulevard is not that bad.

"Tiny Dancer," on that bus, is a spell, an incantation, but a public one, one that also connects the particular congregation to the thousands of like-minded others at diverse sites across the globe. Often the votary will be found in a church of one, singing along with the radio in her bedroom. She belongs to the broader church no less than the desert hermit at prayer among his rocks; the forms link her to it. The words she knows, the tune she hums.

Of course, popular music is democratic in a way poetry's not and probably can't be (even if the reduction of Whitman to a democratic *bonhomme* helps to sell some jeans). "Public" does not equal "everyone." *The Cantos*, for instance, in their magpie hoarding of borrowed song, stage or perform a shareable idiosyncrasy of culture whose elitist ethos does not preclude the expansion of that public, even as that public will lamentably remain foreclosed by accidents of class and education. (What must be democratized is the means of access to art, not art.) In his great essay on Emerson, "Alienated Majesty," Geoffrey Hill mocks the trite notion that poetry's "place is to be supportive of self-improvement and broad ideas of social progress."[11] Do I need to say that by "equipment for living" I do not mean equipment for self-improvement (chicken soup for the soul)?

Frank O'Hara acknowledges the use he makes of poetry by identifying it with his literal equipment for living: "My heart is in my / pocket, it is Poems by Pierre Reverdy." But most people don't seem to need poetry, and, you know, bully for them. Men die miserably every day for lack of clean drinking water and affordable health care, not of what's found in poems. And poetry, alas, can't do a damn thing against capitalism, even as it devotes its intellectual and affective energies to it in a dialectical dance of opposition and complicity. As Joshua Clover says about our claims—whether total or qualified—for "the political force of poetry": "It's such bullshit, isn't it?" Pop is even worse off, a watermarked wing of consumer capitalism structurally restricted to dreams of utopia.

But I take it that our having to ask ourselves what poems and pop songs are *for*, and our compulsion to suggest answers, is a good thing—that it's the fields that are certain of their purpose and their standing that lend themselves most to reified thinking. I mean principally the natural sciences, which shade now so easily into the most preposterous scientism. Evolutionary psychologists will tell you that the arts exist to—well, there's only one reason any human endeavor exists, according to evolutionary psychology. Adam Phillips suggests that it's worth asking what poetry is good for because science is always providing answers to the question what it's good for—vaccines, Google, drone strikes, showrooms filled with fabulous prizes. And for Phillips, poetry—and pop, I'd add—provides a "cure for our pervasive skepticism about whether language works."[12] Whether, that is, the right words can, as psychoanalysis teaches, make us better off.

Phillips's revision of Bloom, then, I might paraphrase as "What can the right language set to music get you out of?" I've no doubt left much undertheorized in this discussion—not least the distinctions

between poetry and pop as equipment for living (I've barely inti-
mated the no-duh role music without words plays in pop). But I hear
Bob Dylan wonder "you have to pay to get out of / going through all
these things twice." Which is to say, to get out of the compulsion to
repeat, which is to say to get out of the death drive (which Phillips
glosses as Freud's way of saying, "we want to die, and whether or
not we want to we will"[13]). Dylan knows there's no getting out of it
at any price, and his song provides in some measure a sad and angry
consolation for this reality. In its strains, as in Freud's and Phillips's
and Hill's, I hear the imperative: *get out of wanting to get out of it*.

And since it would be a cliché to end a chapter on poetry and
pop music with a Dylan quote, let me cite the words of Barry Mann
and Cynthia Weil, made famous by the Animals during the Vietnam
War: "We gotta get out of this place / if it's the last thing we ever do."
Which it will be. But the boulevard is not that bad.

WISCONSIN CHAIR

I remember walking, in my early twenties, in a field in Kansas, listening on my Walkman to a recording of some country-blues compilation. (Norlin Library at the University of Colorado, where I was an indifferent student, used to let you tape any records you wanted from their collection.) It was one of those spots of time you read about in Wordsworth—I mean, there was *nothing* besides sun, dirt, grass, me, and the music. And Richard "Rabbit" Brown's "James Alley Blues" came on. All of Brown's known recordings derive from one session in New Orleans in 1927. But I think "James Alley Blues" must have been sung in the land of Nod, on the east of Eden, in something like the beginning.

The song opens like a pleasant June afternoon as Brown plunks a sweet, lilting melody on his guitar. His high, tattered voice rings out a standard blues:

> Times ain't now nothing like they used to be
> Oh times ain't now nothing like they used to be
> And I'm tellin' you all the truth, oh, take it for me
>
> I done seen better days, but I'm puttin' up with these
> I done seen better days, but I'm puttin' up with these
> I'd have a much better time, but these girls now is so hard
>   to please

It's a marriage plaint—"I'll give you sugar for sugar, let you get salt for salt / And if you can't get 'long with me well it's your own fault." The first time you hear it you fall for it hard, staggered by Brown's dexterity and weird tortoise-shell warble. And then he lands the final couplet and you realize you aren't where you thought you were at all: "Sometimes I think that you too sweet to die / And another time I think you oughta be buried alive."

I played it over and over, pressing rewind and play simultaneously. (Remember that? Chipmunks chittering until you hit the blank space between songs?) I wanted to get all the way around that song, to drop it at my feet like a dead pig, my fang marks in its neck. I wanted to learn its secrets, that I might wield such power myself. I wanted to seduce women. I wanted to be the one to wake people up. I had nowhere to put everything the music made me feel. I still don't.

This insipid breathlessness suggests the differences between how I listened then and how I listen now, twenty years and some joys and many disappointments later. I used to try to listen my way into my skin, but it turned out that listening *was* my skin. Listening to records was not just something I did, it was who I was. Not a day passed, for years, that I didn't spend hours sitting in front of my stereo or burrowing into my Walkman, learning my way around a sound—Coltrane's, Steely Dan's, the Carter Family's, Duke Ellington's, Rakim's.

* * *

Kafka doesn't mention a chair, but one is implied: "There is no need for you to leave the house. Stay at your table and listen. Don't even listen, just wait. Don't even wait, be completely quiet and alone. The world will offer itself to you to be unmasked; it can't do otherwise; in raptures it will writhe before you."

I'm spending a lot of time in my chair as I work my way

through the eight hundred tracks contained in *The Rise and Fall of Paramount Records 1917–1932, Volume 1*—an elaborate $400 box set comprising six "180g vinyl LPs pressed on burled chestnut-colored vinyl with hand-engraved, blind-embossed gold-leaf labels, housed in a laser-etched white birch LP folio," a flash drive loaded with digital files of songs, a clothbound book, hundreds of advertisements and photos, a "field guide" to the 172 artists represented, all of it housed in a handcrafted oak cabinet. The brass flash drive is a replica of the reproducer-and-stylus assembly of the Wisconsin Chair Company's Vista Talking Machine ("The Excellence of Its Quality Makes the Price a Surprise"). The package as an overwhelming whole is too obvious even to serve as an object lesson in conspicuous consumption.

But the music refuses the flamboyance of its housing; in raptures it writhes before me. The stars shine bright—Blind Lemon Jefferson, Ethel Waters, Ma Rainey, Alberta Hunter, Blind Blake—but less bright than lesser lights: the Beale Street Sheiks, Sweet Papa Stovepipe, Lovie Austin, the Herwin Ladies Four. On the Sheiks' "You Shall," an anticlerical acoustic rap version of "You Shall Be Free," Frank Stokes croaks like Redd Foxx ("I don't—'llow my preacher at-my-house-no-more—I don't LIKE 'em—THEY'll rob you") while his and Dan Sane's guitars sparkle and glint off each other.

"You Shall" and many more tracks on the Paramount set take me back to junior high, when a friend introduced me to Robert Johnson and other early American recording artists. Old-timey music, he called it—a kitchen sink rubric encompassing country blues, Dixieland jazz, field recordings, country gospel, ragtime, shouted sermons, jug-band spoon-and-comb combos, hillbilly fiddles, medicine-show blackface yodels. Our holy grail was Harry Smith's *Anthology of American Folk Music*, more heard of than heard in those early CD days, not yet the over-parsed golden calf it's become. Like Enid in Terry Zwigoff's *Ghost World*, returning the needle to the outside groove of Skip James's "Devil Got My Woman" again and again, I listened to some songs so many times I stripped them of meaning and continuity, until they contained only a miscellany of notes, moods, finger-squeaks on strings. I played Johnson's "Me and the Devil Blues" and "Come On in My Kitchen" until I had memorized the very crackles, clicks, and pops of the shellac 78s from which they were transferred. I listened *to* the crackles, clicks, and pops as if they were electronic glitch music.

Hearing these records now is to remember hearing them then. I am in those songs, my idiot dreams tangled up in them. I can no longer hear them without interference, just as New Order's "True Faith" isn't merely a great song I've loved for decades, but the track that dominated my Walkman on the overnight train to Milan when I was twenty-two. It's waking up on that train to find a pretty girl I'd never seen before asleep with her head on my shoulder, mountains and moon in the window, no idea where I was, certain only that anything might happen. It's the recognition that I've now lived nearly twice as long as I had then, and that I'll be lucky to live twice as long as I have now. Every song you loved when you were young turns into "Tintern Abbey."

This is one of the orders of time embraced by popular song. Eric Church's "Springsteen" is about it—"To this day when I hear that song / I see you standing there on that lawn"—as is Taylor Swift's "Tim McGraw," in which the singer hopes a boy will think of her when he hears her favorite song on the radio. This order— call it Springsteenian—is missing from Evan Eisenberg's catalog of musico-temporal architectures in *The Recording Angel*. Eisenberg argues that the phonograph, by making just about any music available to anyone at any time, abolished the ritualized structures of time that music coordinated when it was still perforce a social art. But there are also private times music opens onto: even the most devout medieval churchgoer, instead of attending to the higher time accessed by the Passion, might have found herself replaying her earlier experiences of the music.

Still, recorded music obviously makes these private temporalities more likely. For one thing, the recorded song remains the same.* And a record or MP3 opens a wormhole not only to the girl asleep on the train but to the past time of the recording session itself. I am hearing Geeshie Wiley singing, as John Jeremiah Sullivan recounts, "in the spring of 1930, in a damp and dimly lit studio, in a small Wisconsin village on the western shore of Lake Michigan."[14] I am in that damp and dim space, close to that mystery, searching Wiley's face for signs and revelations. I just sit right here, see her face from the other side.

Live blues in Colorado Springs when I was growing up meant white guys balancing piña coladas on their amps and channeling Mark Knopfler. I learned about the blues from records—and record covers. "Every mode of record listening," Eisenberg writes, "leaves us with a need for something, if not someone, to see and touch. . . . As records tend to look alike and one doesn't want to get fingerprints on them, in practice one adores the album cover."[15] One reason I started paying for music again—buying vinyl again— is that digital music files have nothing to "cover," no sleeve to lose yourself in as you listen. The miniature reproduction of the jacket art that pops up on an iPod or iPhone, smaller than a postage stamp,

---

* Eisenberg: "The phonograph always plays it exactly the same way," unlike a live performer (Evan Eisenberg, *The Recording Angel: Music, Records and Culture from Aristotle to Zappa*, 2nd ed. [New Haven: Yale University Press, 2005], 64). My favorite rock guitar solo is Mick Taylor's at the end of the Stones' "Sway" on *Sticky Fingers*. I immediately noticed when one of the several CD reissues cut the fade-out a fraction of a second early, and couldn't listen to the song on that edition again.

always depresses me a little (as if CD inserts weren't diminished enough).

Like most people who grew up in a house full of records, I spent hours staring at these mystic portals into freakish adult dimensions—a rainbow-haired weirdo smashing himself in the head with an ice-cream cone, a topless young girl holding a silver spacecraft in an endless field of green, green grass. And, once my friend had turned me on to him, a black man seen from above, seated in a plain wooden chair, playing a guitar (you can't see his face; no photographs of Robert Johnson had yet been discovered).

The iconic cover of *King of the Delta Blues Singers* was my first image of the blues. It was soon joined by the cover of *Howlin' Wolf*, semiotically sparer yet somehow more resonant: just an acoustic guitar leaning against a rocking chair. Of course, this is hokey marketing—no acoustic guitar could be heard over the electric snakebite of this record. But the musician's absence clarified a direct relationship of chair to music that made sense to a kid raised by a cheap pair of headphones.

* * *

How a chair company got into the business of producing, under its Paramount Records subsidiary, some of the finest blues and jazz records ever committed to disc is a matter of simple capitalist logic. In 1913, Wisconsin Chair contracted to manufacture wooden cabinets designed to house Edison phonographs. These cabinets were popular. Paramount Records was originally formed to produce loss-leader accessories for them. But Paramount will be remembered as long as people care about Blind Lemon Jefferson's "See That My Grave Is Kept Clean"—as long as people have souls, I guess—and Wisconsin Chair shut down in 1959.

It's always been this way with records: the last shall be first. There is a profoundly boring short film from 1910 called *The Stenographer's Friend, or, What Was Accomplished by an Edison Business*

Phonograph. Having watched all nine minutes, I can vouch for the Library of Congress description:

> It's a busy day at the office, and the stenographer is exhausted from trying to keep up with the demands on her skills. Even when she stays late, she cannot catch up with all of the work. But then a man comes into the office to demonstrate the many advantages of the Edison System, his company's new business phonograph.

The stenographer is so pleased with the invention, which allows her to play back her boss's dictation for transcription, that she smilingly pats the phonograph as if it were a Shih Tzu.

This is the sort of use Edison envisioned for his creation—business correspondence. It didn't occur to him that anyone might listen to music on the thing.* This has always seemed as remarkable to me as if he'd invented the chair and supposed that folks might use it mainly as a stepladder. I would have immediately thought of recording Verdi's "Ah, fors' è lui" or hillbilly tunes in central Kentucky.

Except I wouldn't have, because we're historical sedimentation and root architecture, and I wouldn't be the particular *I* I am if the record player didn't exist. If I look at a talking box and think music,

---

* Edison also, of course, thought wax cylinders would make better records than flat discs, partly because he didn't foresee a need for ease of storage: you just shaved down the wax after listening and reused the cylinder. He did include "reproduction of music" fourth on a list of possible uses for the phonograph published in 1878, between "the teaching of elocution" and "the 'Family Record'—a registry of sayings, reminiscences, etc., by members of a family in their own voices, and of the last words of dying persons." But he believed the device would be used primarily to reproduce speech, and marketed it accordingly.

it's because I've spent my life playing music on talking boxes. That might seem obvious, but it's not. In a material sense, anyone could have built a phonograph centuries before Edison—you just need a stylus, some foil, and copper. But as Friedrich Kittler argues, you also need "the historical a priori of sound recording," the "immaterials of scientific origin, which are not so easy to come by and have to be supplied by a science of the soul."[16] In 1806, the English naturalist Thomas Young figured out how to record the vibrations of a tuning fork on a wax-covered rotating drum; in 1857, a French bookseller named Édouard-Léon Scott de Martinville modified Young's device. His "phonautograph" transcribed the human voice into squiggles. But it didn't occur to either man to try to play these recordings back. Why not?* Edison himself didn't even mean to invent the phonograph; he was experimenting with ways to record telegraphic and telephonic messages—trying to create voice mail, basically.

Kittler claims that both scientific ideology (an emphasis on acoustic frequencies rather than musical intervals) and technical limitations (music would really come into its own with the advent of electrical recording) prevented Edison from thinking of the phonograph as a contribution to the history of music. It's true that Edison appears to have been especially doltish where music was concerned. But he *had* to fail to foresee just how his invention would revolutionize human experience. He was simply embedded in history. Like us.

Early on, as is apparent from the word itself, phonography was conceived as a form of writing, as photography had been—but a form that couldn't be "read": Edison spent hours trying to find the

---

* In 2008, a team of scientists successfully converted an 1860 phonautogram— the wavy lines the phonautograph scored into sooty paper—of Scott singing "Au clair de la lune" into sound. You can hear it on YouTube.

letter *a* in the grooves of a record. An analogy was drawn between phonographic inscription and hieroglyphics, which resisted legibility for centuries.[17] It feels right, then, that phonography should begin in missed connections and secretarial dreams. In a lovely conceit, the poet Jack Gilbert resists the historical a priori of writing's similar birth as transactional notation:

> When the thousands
> of mysterious Sumerian tablets were translated,
> they seemed to be business records. But what if they
> are poems or psalms? My joy is the same as twelve
> Ethiopian goats standing silent in the morning light.
> O Lord, thou art slabs of salt and ingots of copper,
> as grand as ripe barley lithe under the wind's labor.

Is human mundanity ever far from any source of the marvelous?

* * *

Edison's phonograph becomes Berliner's gramophone; a chair company wants to sell cabinets; record scouts fan out across the South. Popular music is a commodity.

This circumstance, Elijah Wald argues in *Escaping the Delta*, shapes and distorts our perceptions of the recording era—makes marvelous the mundane. No one bought the handful of sides Son House cut for Paramount, so he recorded no more in his prime, and we're left with an American lacuna on the order of Archilochos's lost poems. Juke joints in prewar Clarksdale played the latest hits, including Glenn Miller and Bing Crosby, not the hellhound howls of the fabled Delta blues. Robert Johnson didn't sell his soul, he listened to records. No one even *thought* he sold his soul, that was a joke, a way of saying *that cat could play*. Wald would hear the blues unalloyed, without "the filter of rock 'n' roll and our own modern tastes."[18] He's like someone explaining a magic trick—you're supposed to come away from his research with a chastened appreciation of Johnson's music.

But the explanations have the effect of redoubling your astonishment—how did Johnson get *that* from *this*? I feel like a class traitor for saying so, but the most scrupulous historicism leaves a remainder in the highest art—a residue we used to attribute to "genius" or "soul." And Wald just isn't the writer to get at that residue. He reduces "Hellhound on My Trail" to a pile of clichés: "It is the cry of an ancient mariner, cursed by his fates and doomed to range eternally through the world without hope of port or savior."[19] Compare Greil Marcus, tracing Johnson's shadow to America's Puritan dawn: "Because of our faith in promises, the true terror of doom is in the American's natural inability to believe doom is real, even when he knows it has taken over his life. When there is no way to speak of terror and no one to listen if there were, Johnson's songs matter."[20]

Wald's guff about ancient mariners is exactly the wrong image for Johnson's sound, which Marcus rightly locates in the land. While both critics hear doom in the music, only Marcus has specified an emotional reality. Wald sounds like someone trying to find high-flown words for a generic experience; Marcus has listened to the songs, and is troubled by the conclusions he's been forced to draw.

The point is that Wald's fidelity to historical fact leaves little room for aesthetic truth. Popular music is a commodity that is not identical with itself, riven by contradiction. Thus Marcus's answer to Wald's objections, almost thirty years before he made them:

What Robert Johnson had to do with other bluesmen of his time is interesting to me, but not nearly so interesting as what Johnson has to do with those discovering him now, without warning and on their own. The original context of Johnson's story is important, and it is where his story is usually placed; but a critic's job is not only to define the context of an artist's work but to expand that context, and it seems more important to me that Johnson's music is vital enough to enter other contexts and create all over again.[21]

Both writers are sensitive to the ways records create their own contexts, unmoored from their conditions of production. Only Marcus is interested in the teenaged me, spinning a sound I can't reach the bottom of on my dad's JVC turntable.

* * *

I listened differently in those days, of course. So did you, if you've ever been sixteen (some people, I noticed then, skip right from puberty to adulthood). I listened for clues to who I was. I found them, or I didn't, or not finding them was the clue I needed. I thought that if I could say, with Johnson on "Me and the Devil Blues," "Baby, I don't care where you bury my body when I'm dead and gone," I would be free—of what, I didn't know.

The music I heard on turntables and CD players and tape decks made me believe that anything was possible, that the quintessential American sentence could be finished, that I could finish it: "It eluded us then, but that's no matter—tomorrow we will run faster, stretch out our arms farther. . . . And then one fine morning—"

Well, that's a hell of a thing for any invention to make a body believe, much less one that was meant to improve business efficiency. And it's a silly thing to believe, based in misreadings. But it's true that now all I get from music is music—a way of thinking and feeling, sure, but not a way of living. Records are useful equipment *for* living, provided you don't expect more from them than they contain. I sit here in my chair listening on my headphones to old Paramount sides, or the country gospel of the Reverend Gary Davis, and I'm still transmitted to the past, seeing the faces from the other side. But the future's no longer part of the picture, and every sentence ends in an em dash.

Which, of course, is the point. Other gifts have followed.

* * *

And yet records aren't the whole story. Dom Gregory Dix, in his classic *The Shape of the Liturgy*, lamented the decline of the corporate worship of the Eucharist "into a mere focus for the subjective devotion of each separate worshipper in the isolation of his own mind."[22] Sometimes I need an order larger than the self in its chair, sealed off from the broader church. Of course, this now gets mediated in weird ways. John Jeremiah Sullivan writes of Michael Jackson's lip-synched performance of "Billie Jean" on NBC's *Motown 25* that it was "possibly the most captivating thing a person's ever been captured doing onstage."[23] I remember seeing that performance in 1983, feeling that I was somehow connected to my schoolmates watching in their homes, imagining what we'd say about it in the halls the next day.

In 2014, I was half watching the Grammys on television, skimming through my Twitter feed. Taylor Swift came out to perform "All Too Well," and I put down my laptop to check her out. It was—well, cards on the table, I think it was transcendent. Someone forgot to tell her the Grammys are a joke. She got her Stevie Nicks on, banging her locks and singing pretty much in key, hunched over the piano like a velociraptor and tearing the meat off its bones. On record, the song is one of her best, but on that night, on my television screen, for as long as it lasted, it was the best song I'd ever heard. After, as the applause swelled, she cast a stony lizard gaze on the assembled royalty as if she'd forgotten who they were. As if she was sure they hadn't learned a thing. I couldn't believe what I'd just witnessed, and, turning back to Twitter, I saw that no one else could either.

But the not-quite-illusory connectedness hawked by media corporations is still a wispy simulacrum compared to gathering with strangers at a club or concert hall to hear a band. Not long ago, I saw Jason Moran's trio at the Village Vanguard. He was on his Fats Waller kick—giant papier-mâché mask, looped samples. His version of "Jitterbug Waltz" brought me to tears. I was with a friend, and we had been talking earlier in the evening about our attraction to disparate accounts of the world as broken—Marxism, Christianity. I leaned across to her during the song and said, "The world is broken, but this is one of the things we do about it," gesturing in awe at the group. She said, "And would it mean as much if the world were whole?" Which is basically the theme of this book. And I'm sure all that sounds ridiculous, but "Jitterbug Waltz" was incandescent and perfect that night. I bought Moran's record, took it home, put on his studio version of the song. It wasn't even close.

"

HOLES

2-XL wasn't a real robot, just a cheap eight-track player, a toy, vaguely shaped like R2-D2. It came with interactive educational eight-track cartridges (if you're under thirty, your childhood was less technologically exasperating than mine). I mostly played music on it—Billy Joel, the Eagles, Journey. Someone, when I was around eight years old, gave me *Sgt. Pepper's Lonely Hearts Club Band.*

The ones that got me were "Being for the Benefit of Mr. Kite!" and "A Day in the Life." Spooky melodies, weird breaks—they reminded me of church music. I'd stare at the cover—on an eight-track, a tiny piece of paper glued to a chunk of plastic—while I listened to the songs. I had questions. Who were the Hendersons? What was a hogshead, exactly? (It couldn't be what it sounded like—on fire?) But most important: What could it mean to "know how many holes it takes to fill the Albert Hall"? I ran that line through my mind every which way. My dad explained the Albert Hall: big concert hall, London. But the eeriness of the line wasn't dispelled, because there's no sense in which "holes" can "fill" anything, and because of the long lilting hole-filled sound of the line: *now – know – how – hole – fill – Al – hall.*

I don't even much like *Sgt. Pepper's* now. But I'll never get to the bottom of "A Day in the Life." *Now they know how many holes it takes to fill the Albert Hall.* It's a metaphor: for what, though? You don't decide to go deep into words; something takes you there—a plastic robot, Lennon-McCartney—something that says *I'd love to turn you on.*

* * *

A movie on TV. Two men are sitting by a campfire. One of them begins freakishly to intone. The words—I have no idea what they mean, but I'm bewitched. When they finish falling, the speaker turns to his companion and says, "Yeats."

I don't remember what the movie was or what lines the actor quoted. I was fourteen or so, and all I knew about William Butler Yeats was that he said things fall apart, and I knew that because I'd read Stephen King's *The Stand*. But I hadn't realized poetry could do *this* to you—could bind you with a spell and leave you feeling like your dog just died.

I checked out *The Collected Poems of W. B. Yeats* from my high school library in Colorado Springs and never returned it. I started reading at the beginning, so the first Yeats poem I ever read wasn't "The Second Coming" or "Leda and the Swan" or "The Lake Isle of Innisfree," it was "The Song of the Happy Shepherd." I took its principle that "Words alone are certain good" a bit too seriously.

"The Rose of Peace" was the first poem I ever memorized. I would chant it to myself while walking in my grandparents' pasture in Rose Hill, Kansas, petting the horses, not always avoiding their apples. Here's the opening:

> If Michael, leader of God's host
> When Heaven and Hell are met,
> Looked down on you from Heaven's door-post
> He would his deeds forget.
>
> Brooding no more upon God's wars
> In his divine homestead,
> He would go weave out of the stars
> A chaplet for your head.

I didn't yet know to call this ballad meter, but its cadences rolled through me. I read Yeats's poems for days, often without understanding a word. It was my first real immersion in poetry, and this auditory intelligence rewired me. Imagine if the first movie you ever saw was *Madame de* . . . .

Decades later, Yeats's pitch still seems to me better than any other poet's I know. And that fact still seems mysterious, though it has something to do with repetition and variation. Often, like Qoheleth, Yeats will build and build until his rhetoric reaches a boiling point, at which point the poem begins to pick up and resituate words and phrases in a way that, at the moment, makes me think of Anna Kendrick playing "The Cup Song" in *Pitch Perfect*:

> Hearts with one purpose alone
> Through summer and winter seem
> Enchanted to a stone
> To trouble the living stream.
> The horse that comes from the road,
> The rider, the birds that range
> From cloud to tumbling cloud,
> Minute by minute they change;
> A shadow of cloud on the stream
> Changes minute by minute;
> A horse-hoof slides on the brim,
> And a horse plashes within it;
> The long-legged moor-hens dive,
> And hens to moor-cocks call;
> Minute by minute they live:
> The stone's in the midst of all.

Here, in "Easter, 1916," the shifts are mimetic of what they describe, the antimetabolic movement from "Minute by minute they change" to "Changes minute by minute," the incremental recalibrations of stone and stream, horse and cloud. Yeats recurs to these incantatory effects—chiasmus, antimetabole, and simple repetition—again and again throughout his poetry.

When I first noticed this all those years ago—"They came like swallows and like swallows went"; "I call it death-in-life and life-in-death"; "I have a marvellous thing to say, / A certain marvellous thing"—I thought it a great discovery. Later I learned there have been many studies of this crucial feature of Yeats's rhetoric. I am not sure, though, that anyone has noted a possible provenance in these lines of Lionel Johnson's, quoted by Yeats in a late essay:

> The Saints in golden vesture shake before the gale;
> The glorious windows shake, where still they dwell
>   enshrined;
> Old Saints by long-dead, shriveled hands, long since
>   designed:
> There still, although the world autumnal be, and pale,
> Still in their golden vesture the old Saints prevail

Hearing Johnson recite this poem deeply affected the younger Yeats, and I suspect he took from it perhaps more than it contains.

It was not then my intention to study Yeats, at least not in a scholarly sense, but to listen to him, to repeat his words to myself, dropping them among the horses' droppings. And though my own work fails to measure up to my great example in every way, this is how I learned to write: read and recite, recite and read, repeat.

" "

JOURNEY FORCE

Amid camera trickery at least as advanced as Louis Lumière's in *Démolition d'un mur*, Steve Perry is emoting backward through stacks of shipping pallets. It's the video for Journey's 1983 hit "Separate Ways (Worlds Apart)." He lip-synchs over arena-synth bombast: "Promises we made were in vain—in VAY-ay-ay-een, *VAY-een*!" At about the 2:21 mark, he glances behind him to make sure he's not about to smack into something. Journey was a band too heedlessly excited about its dumbest ideas to prefer choreography to contusions.

From the fifth through seventh grades, I was a card-carrying member of Journey Force, the band's official fan club (they issued you a card; I carried it). Every month I devoured the official Journey Force newsletter, *Journey Force*, which ran hard-hitting interviews with band members:

> **Journey Force:** Congratulations on your Grammy nominations! How does it feel to be nominated?
>
> **Steve Perry:** God, it's amazing! I'm so excited. I was nominated for my participation in "We Are the World" and I'm in there for a single ("If Only for the Moment, Girl"), and possibly for the album of the year. I think there's also a category for "Best Performance By a Group or Duo."
>
> **Journey Force:** That must be really exciting. Are you going to the ceremonies?

Steve Perry: Yes! I've got my tuxedo coming in, with tails and everything. Speaking of tails, we're discussing selling a T-shirt at the Journey concerts that has tails . . . it's black and a T-shirt, but it has tails. We were talking about that at the meeting today.

Now that's what I call a meeting.

I had several Journey T-shirts, without tails, as well as Journey headbands and Journey wristbands (it was the '80s). Journey pins adorned my jacket—one depicting the cover of the album *Escape* (a scarab spaceship exploding from its chrysalis planet), one the disconcerting blue robot head (or whatever it is) from the cover of *Frontiers*. I tracked down all the albums on cassette, even the pre-Perry waste products—*Journey*, *Look into the Future*, and *Next*—and guitarist Neal Schon's solo emetic with Sammy Hagar. I had the *Journey Escape* video game for the Atari 2600, a cynical product of rock corporatism apparently designed to kill Lester Bangs. (After "a spectacular performance," you have to lead the band members to the scarab spaceship thing while *protecting the concert cash* from "hordes of Love-Crazed Groupies, Sneaky Photographers, and Shifty-Eyed Promoters," as the game manual puts it. There was an arcade game, too, but I never played it or even saw it in an arcade—in this version, fans steal the band's instruments and hide them on various planets. "It's such a pleasurable experience to meet [our fans]," Perry told *Journey Force* in 1984.)

All this meant I had negative cultural capital at Woodland Park Middle School. Girls liked Journey. Guys, committed to the masculinist overdrive of football and pushing nerds into lockers, listened to Iron Maiden and Ozzy. Being mocked for liking the wrong bands was part of the natural noise of my childhood, so normal I didn't question it. Anyway, I bonded with metal girls over Journey (Nikki Wright, get at me).

I must've known at some level that Journey wasn't considered "good"—was, in fact, considered a joke. But I wasn't aware that such a thing as music criticism existed, so I hadn't heard of Robert Christgau, whose D+ review of *Frontiers* would have infuriated me: "Just a reminder, for all who believe the jig is really up this time, of how much worse things might be: this top ten album could be outselling *Pyromania*, or *Flashdance*, or even *Thriller*." Possessing a nervous system, Christgau loved *Thriller*, but the other two mentions were digs: *Even this crap is better than Journey*. (At the time, I owned all four albums, and I still say Def Leppard's *Pyromania* is a goddamn masterpiece.)

It was only much later that I began to care what smart writers thought about music I loved—or that I had foolishly believed I loved, but I couldn't have loved what Greil Marcus called "the self-evident phoniness in Steve Perry's voice—the oleaginous self-regard, the gooey smear of words, the horrible enunciation," right? If I loved all that, then I must have bad taste.

Eventually, of course, I did succumb to right thinking. My family moved to Colorado Springs, where I fell in with skateboarders, who turned me on to Black Flag, Minor Threat, Big Black, the Minutemen. From there it was but a short step to the usual constructed ideas of *good taste in music*. My first thought was to list a bunch of artists here to prove my credentials, which just shows how deeply these identitarian impulses run. For years, my younger sister would, to embarrass me, bring up my preadolescent fandom. I pretended my infatuation with Journey had been an elaborate, ironic gag, which drove her crazy.

So let me make it up to her by affirming now, without irony: I like Journey. Or, at least, I like two Journey songs (not counting Steve Perry's magnificent solo hits "Oh Sherrie" and "Foolish Heart"). I first heard "Only the Young," Journey's second-best song, in 1985, when I bought the matchless *Vision Quest* soundtrack on cassette at a Sears in Colorado Springs. Later I would learn the band left it off *Frontiers* in favor of two forgettable tracks. Of course. The song roars to life with Schon's pick slide, and Perry's off in the ether, belting needlework-sampler wisdom poetry. "Only the young can say," because the young see through "promises" and "lies." The synths and processed guitars swell like a mammoth wheel of Monterey Jack left in the sun.

I'm supposed to be repelled by this, but I find it thrilling. The intervening years of tasteful discrimination haven't blunted its power. "Only the Young" distills Journey's message, insofar as the band was coherent enough to have one: *the kids are all right, they just wanna be free*. It's there in "Escape," amid hair-metal riffs avant la leather—a kid's "breakin' all the rules" and "gettin' out from this masquerade." It's there in the titles of the group's best-known records: *Departure, Escape, Frontiers*. It's a perfectly generic message, expressed without humor or poetry, but it becomes something more in Journey's one great song, full stop.

You can't listen to "Don't Stop Believin'" now without thinking of Tony Soprano, who punches it on the jukebox before the screen goes dark in the most overanalyzed scene in television history. It's an inspired choice—a synecdoche for Tony's lack of sophistication, his humanity. If Scorsese had filmed it, Tony would've played "Gimme Shelter" or something. But instead, here's this very bad guy whom you care about because you've been immersed in his life for six seasons—"the most fully drawn person in modern fiction," David Thomson called him—and you're never going to see him again, and the poignancy and strangeness of that are wrapped up in a hackneyed corporate-schlock anthem.

At least that's what you're supposed to think "Don't Stop Believin'" is. Punk and its aftermath made high school bearable for me, but it also wiped some of the best bands of the '70s and '80s and their songs off the board for self-consciously cool kids. I sometimes dream of a world where my generation worshiped Van Halen instead of the Pixies. Journey wasn't one of those bands, but "Don't Stop Believin'" is one of those songs. It cascades from *whoosh* to *whoosh*—it peaks all the way down, closer to a twenty-first-century pop hit like Amerie's "1 Thing" than to similar-souled stadium ballads like Styx's "Come

Sail Away." Like its "small town girl" and "city boy from South Detroit"—a section of Detroit that exists only in the mind of Steve Perry ("the syntax just sounded right," he said)—the song might go anywhere, do anything, as long as it's somewhere *bigger*, something *gaudier*. As Chris Willman wrote for the *Los Angeles Times* music blog:

> Structurally, it's a mess: Surely one would get tossed out of songwriting school for a tune that follows its opening piano riff with a verse, a guitar arpeggio, a second verse, a bridge, a guitar solo, a third verse, a repeat of the bridge, another guitar solo . . . and then, 3 minutes, 20 seconds in, when the song is ready to fade out, one of the most unforgettable choruses in rock.

Songwriting school? Not in South Detroit, brother. Just as bands like Talking Heads and Buzzcocks were tightening anxiety-wired rock songs, Journey went full-barrel baroque for bliss.

Maybe I wouldn't hear so much in the song now if I hadn't lip-synched it into my air-mike so much then. I remember waiting impatiently for the band to play "Don't Stop Believin'" the one time I saw them live, at Denver's McNichols Sports Arena in 1986. My dad, reluctant chaperone, was more interested in their opening act, the Outfield, who'd ridden the bad vibes of "Your Love" onto an NPR program he'd heard. His interest didn't survive their first song. I asked him recently if he remembered anything specific about the concert, and he said, "I remember specifically that I was bored."

Journey did play the song, of course, and I was big with wonder.

In a few years I'd be standing with friends in much smaller and grimier venues, watching bands like the Butthole Surfers, the Replacements, Warlock Pinchers, and Sonic Youth, and Journey would be an embarrassment. In 2000, they paved McNichols Sports Arena and put up a parking lot. But as I listen to "Don't Stop Believin'" today, once again, in the arena of my soul, how high that highest Bic lights the dark.

"

THE CHILD THAT SUCKETH LONG

They appear to be the names of heavy metal bands: Plague of Fables; Star-Flanked Seed; Serpent Caul; Murder of Eden; Altar of Plagues; Seed-at-Zero; The Grave and My Calm Body; Dark Asylum; Mares of Thrace; Herods Wail; Christbread; Binding Moon; Red Swine. In fact they are phrases culled from Dylan Thomas's poems—except that I threw two actual metal bands in there. Didn't notice, did you? The best metal undercuts its portentousness with self-awareness—if your major tropes include corpse paint and Satanism, you'd better not take yourself too seriously. In Thomas's work, self-seriousness *is* the major trope. There's wit, but little humor. All those moons, loves, deaths, *O*s. Everything is intoned from on high: "Death is all metaphors, shape in one history," he tells us: "The child that sucketh long is shooting up." Wouldn't you?

Those lines are from "Altarwise by Owl-light," the poem that most haunted me in my teens, largely because I just could not tell what the fuck it was about, a confusion not terribly alleviated by Thomas's own explication, which I discovered in my high school library: "Those sonnets are only the writings of a boily boy in love with shapes and shadows on his pillow. . . . They would be of interest to another boily boy. Or a boily girl. Boily-girly."

It's probably his greatest performance, so it has the highest ratio of smashing lines to the kind of thing you'd expect unicorns to write:

> This was the sky, Jack Christ, each minstrel angle
> Drove in the heaven-driven of the nails
> Till the three-coloured rainbow from my nipples
> From pole to pole leapt round the snail-waked world.

If you don't like "This was the sky, Jack Christ" or "snail-waked world," you don't like poetry. And if you can get the image of *rainbows* shooting out of pudgy-faced Dylan Thomas's *nipples* out of your mind anytime soon, you've got a heaven-driven hole in your head.

There is a quirkiness to Thomas's disregard for what part of speech a word usually is that at its best recalls Stevens—"A grief ago" is instantly, telescopically parsable. But at its worst, well—"I fellowed sleep who kissed me in the brain, / Let fall the tear of time" sounds like E. E. Cummings. In fact, Thomas's lumpier excrescences usually recall no one so much as Cummings in his twilight-wristed cups: the willy-nilly word order, the grammatical burps, the nonsense masquerading as secular scripture. Of course Thomas is a better poet than Cummings (who isn't?), but they are similarly susceptible to the smear of sentimentality:

> No. Not for Christ's dazzling bed
> Or a nacreous sleep among soft particles and charms
> My dear would I change my tears or your iron head.
> Thrust, my daughter or son, to escape, there is none, none,
>   none,
> Nor when all ponderous heaven's host of waters breaks.

Who does the guy think he is? I wouldn't change anyone's head for a higher thread count, either. The allusion to Gerard Manley Hopkins's "No worst, there is none" feels unearned: Hopkins sincerely believed the state of his soul was at stake. All that's at stake for Thomas is whether his self-pity has been gorgeously enough expressed.

And it has. That's what I hate most about Thomas: if you care about poems, you can't entirely hate him. Phrases, images, metaphors rise from the precious muck and lodge themselves in you like shrapnel. "And the dust shall sing like a bird / As the grains blow"; "The sundering ultimate kingdom of genesis' thunder"; "the kangaroo foot of the earth"; "Always goodbye to the long-legged bread"; "The whole of the moon I could love and leave"; "And one light's language in the book of trees"; "When, like a running grave, time tracks you down"; "I make a weapon of an ass's skeleton"; "where maggots have their X"; "the synagogue of the ear of corn"; "famous among the barns."

Like Hart Crane's, Thomas's faults protrude embarrassingly from the wazoo. Crane's are a little easier to forgive, since he had vision, and Thomas was myopic. But at his best he has, like Crane, a towering presence of mind, a stranglehold on the language. Perhaps I'd love him more if I hadn't loved him so much so early. I've made my peace with other early crushes who came to seem so much mannered mush: James Wright, Rilke, Neruda. Rereading Thomas now, I find myself thawing toward him, as I slowly did toward those others, whom now I love anew, love more clearly. So get you gone, Dylan Thomas, though with blessings on your head.

DESTROY YOUR SAFE AND HAPPY LIVES

In the beginning, William Blake writes a gonzo mythos called *Milton*:

> All that can be annihilated must be annihilated
> That the Children of Jerusalem may be saved from slavery
> There is a Negation, & there is a Contrary
> The Negation must be destroyd to redeem the Contraries
> The Negation is the Spectre; the Reasoning Power in Man
> This is a false Body: an Incrustation over my Immortal
> Spirit; a Selfhood, which must be put off & annihilated
>   alway

In another beginning, a bunch of working-class drug users detune their guitars and add some horror-flick spookiness to the blues. Metal—no one can agree on when or why the "heavy" fell off—is born, half in love with easeful death, with Rimbaud's "chaos of ice and polar night," which could describe the sound of a record like the Norwegian black metal band Immortal's *Sons of Northern Darkness*.*

---

* A note on terminology: the tag "heavy metal" was applied to various psychedelic and/or blues-based rock bands throughout the '60s and early '70s, but it seems to have stuck when Lester Bangs used it to describe Led

These two histories probably have no connection besides the one they spark in me, even if "All that can be annihilated must be annihilated" could be every metal band's credo, precisely because the line is a sort of affirmation—destruction in the name of redemption.* But this is how popular music works: in secret histories and self-contained channels. As John Ashbery says, "The songs decorate our notion of the world / And mark its limits."

Metal and poetry are, among other things, arts of accusation and instruction. Together with Rilke's archaic torso of Apollo, they say:

Zeppelin and Black Sabbath, by broad consensus the first (and perhaps the best) heavy metal bands. As rock and roll became rock, heavy metal yielded to metal—splintering into a kajillion subgenres ranging from cough-syrup slow to so fast that drummers use electronic triggers to produce uniform beats at tempos faster than is normally possible with human arms and legs. Genre classification doesn't interest me. Listen to Poison Idea's *Feel the Darkness* followed by Repulsion's *Horrified*, and tell me the main difference between hardcore punk and metal isn't that one has a bullshit positive message and the other has a bullshit negative message. Hell, I think Steely Dan is metal half the time. But for the record, here's a breakdown of some of the most popular metal subgenres. *Thrash metal* is fast and angry; practitioners often appear to have spent too much time lifting weights. *Death metal* comes from Florida, is superfast, and sometimes employs meters more often associated with jazz, or at least with Weather Report; lyrics tend to be about death and dying and killing. *Black metal* is from Norway, sounds like Joy Division on Benzedrine, and won't shut up about Satan; these are the idiots who burned dozens of churches, some centuries old. *Doom metal* is low and slow, sometimes to the point of sounding like Pauline Oliveros, and mainly concerns the relationship between despair and marijuana.

* Of course, Blake urges "mental fight" in the name of an idiosyncratically militant Christianity, whereas metal tends to be Christ-centric in, um, a slightly different way. But the marshaling of spiritual resources against Reason's temples of destruction finds surprising resonance in the visions of technocratic nightmare common to certain strains of metal (e.g., the Québécois band Voivod's entire oeuvre).

"You must change your life." To see metal as demanding something of us—a fundamental change, a shift in perspective, an acknowledgment that we are *headed in the wrong direction*—is to acknowledge that when we listen to it, we're receptive to its message. ("I beg you to listen," Ashbery writes. "You are already listening.") But metal's message is not the same thing as its rhetoric.

Metal's most familiar trope is, duh, Satanism, which might be silly—okay, it's definitely silly—but has a distinguished literary pedigree. Romantic diabolism since the nineteenth century has taken its cue from Milton's *Paradise Lost*. "Milton's Devil as a moral being," wrote Percy Bysshe Shelley, is "far superior to his God." Blake said Milton was "of the Devil's party without knowing it." In the twentieth century, this view of Milton was charmingly defended by William Empson, who argued, more or less, that if by the end of the poem Satan is a rather unsympathetic character, it's only because God's such a jerk.

Whatever one thinks of this interpretation—and most modern critics reject it—it's clear that Satan has the best lines:

> That we were formed, then, say'st thou? and the work
> Of secondary hands, by task transferred
> From Father to his Son? Strange point and new!
> Doctrine which we would know whence learned: who saw
> When this creation was? Remember'st thou
> Thy making, while the Maker gave thee being?
> We know no time when we were not as now;
> Know none before us, self-begot, self-raised
> By our own quickening power . . .

For Shelley, it is Satan's "energy and magnificence" in such passages that mark his superiority. A similar energy inspired Lord Byron, whose epigones Robert Southey dubbed, to Byron's evident delight, the Satanic School. And a bit later, in the France of the Second Empire, Charles Baudelaire would write a prayer to the "loveliest" angel, "a God betrayed, to whom no anthems rise": "O Satan, take pity on my sore distress!"*

Well, Old Scratch has more anthems by now than he knows what to do with. And of course Satanism in metal—from Black Sabbath (some of whose early lyrics are actually kind of Christian) to the goofy Swedish pop-metal band Ghost, whose members dress as skeleton popes and devils—is just theater, a metaphor for nonconformity that affirms dark, creative energies that orthodox political-religious-scientific thought would repress. A few black metal bands profess a dully literal belief in Satanism, but I'm not convinced they're actually interested in anything besides adolescent provocation. As the poet Brandon Brown writes in his obnoxious pseudo-translation of *Les Fleurs du mal*:

> I'd worship Satan
> if only I weren't so allergic to the monochrome
> gloomy sartorial orthodoxy
> and Nordic vibrato of its brutal soundtrack.

You can quibble with his reading of black metal, but Brown's point is well taken: Satanism is boring.

* * *

More seductive is another trope derived from Romanticism, metal's enthralling evocation of nature as a sublime and eerie prophylactic against "killing technology," as Voivod has it. This can get silly too: when I saw them in the summer of 2012, Agalloch had little shrines of animal bones set up on the merch table. Aaron Weaver,

---

* "To whom no anthems rise" is Richard Howard's version of Baudelaire's more straightforward "*privé de louanges*." "Rise" is a nice touch.

the drummer and songwriter for Wolves in the Throne Room, once said that the group's black metal is inspired by "the moss, the roots and the trees, and the animals that live around here, and the weather and the natural forces that human beings encounter."[24] You expect him to try to sell you some beads. But when, on the band's "Prayer of Transformation," Nathan Weaver screams out of a shoegazing guitar haze, "Lay your corpse upon a nest of oak leaves . . . A vessel awaits built from owl feathers and moss," it's no longer merely silly, because the sound is overpowering, majestic, soothing and threatening at once, like a pretty dentist's assistant slipping the mask over your face. I imagine a band playing in some natural old-growth cathedral, overtones crashing into boulders and echoing off ferns.

The apotheosis of this pagan current is reached in the video for Immortal's "Call of the Wintermoon," which suggests an infernal collaboration between Caspar David Friedrich and Walt Disney. The band members, dressed as wizards, scamper about in an impossibly green forest, breathing fire and posing dramatically in time with the song's relentless clatter, which sounds a bit like one of those apps that play rain sounds while you sleep, except with someone croaking semi-comprehensibly about "winterwings" and "Northern darkness." It's both embarrassingly inane and, somehow, genuinely evocative of an eerie wilderness sublime, a hokey reminder of why the Puritans of early New England associated the forest with the devil. These corpse-painted Gandalfs are late for a black mass with Hawthorne's Goody Cloyse.

Black metal's romantic fetishization of nature is—like Satanism, really—an "angry lament for human folly," as Erik Davis puts it in an article for *Slate* on Wolves in the Throne Room ("Evil is the nature of mankind," the devil tells Goodman Brown).[25] It's a mystic-igloo version of Wordsworth's "The world is too much with us"—

> Little we see in Nature that is ours;
> We have given our hearts away, a sordid boon!
> This Sea that bares her bosom to the moon;

The winds that will be howling at all hours,
And are up-gathered now like sleeping flowers;
For this, for everything, we are out of tune;
It moves us not.

—and just as didactic-mournful in its way as the sardonic eco-rage
of a poet like Juliana Spahr:

> We let the runoff from agriculture, surface mines, forestry,
> home wastewater treatment systems, construction sites,
> urban yards, and roadways into our hearts.

> We let chloride, magnesium, sulfate, manganese, iron,
> nitrite/nitrate, aluminum, suspended solids, zinc,
> phosphorus, fertilizers, animal wastes, oil, grease, dioxins,
> heavy metals, and lead go through our skin and into our
> tissues.

> We were born at the beginning of these things, at the time of
> chemicals combining, at the time of stream run off.
> These things were a part of us and would become more a
> part of us but we did not know it yet.

> Still we noticed enough to sing a lament.[26]

Metal's iconography—devil horns, pagan altars, blood on the
forest floor—embraces the dark and primordial; it's a rebuke to our
soft lives.* We are, metal says, "out of tune." Deathspell Omega, a

---

* The German philosopher Peter Sloterdijk paraphrases Rilke's directive
as "Give up your attachment to comfortable ways of living" in *You Must
Change Your Life* (Cambridge, UK: Polity Press, 2013), 28.

wonderfully pretentious French black metal band (their latest album titles are in Latin), quote Georges Bataille: "Every human being not going to the extreme limit is the servant or the enemy of man and the accomplice of a nameless obscenity." Which sounds like a translation back into English of a bad translation into French of one of Blake's "Proverbs of Hell." I'm surprised more bands haven't plundered this treasure house: "Sooner murder an infant in its cradle than nurse unacted desires"; "The lust of the goat is the bounty of God"; "The road of excess leads to the palace of wisdom"; "The tygers of wrath are wiser than the horses of instruction"; "Drive your cart and your plow over the bones of the dead." Sounds pretty metal to me.

Although metal lyrics provide a trove of such sentiments, no one should listen to metal for the lyrics, which are mostly unskillful. They're also mostly indecipherable, so no matter. (Yes, there are plenty of exceptions—smart lyrics, clear vocals, both at the same time. I said "mostly.") Metal makes its argument viscerally. It's "a triumph of vulgarity, velocity," says the music critic Chuck Eddy, with "no redeeming social value."[27]

Erik Danielsson, frontman for the Swedish black metal outfit Watain, told me that metal "is the form of music through which Diabolical energies flow with the most swiftness and potency." All metal is a variation on two themes: loud and fast. Some songs are quiet and slow, but always against the background of normative loudness and speed. (Punk and free jazz are loud and fast too, but metal is louder, faster, and less wholesome.)

That said, what always has to be emphasized to metal skeptics is that, as Eddy writes, "it really *doesn't* 'all sound the same.' By now it's more varied than any other white-rock genre." If you never listen to something, it's easy to say it all sounds the same. But Guns N' Roses' tuneful boogie doesn't sound at all like Converge's war punk. You can hear Iron Maiden's guitar trellises in Carcass's jet-engine revs, but you'd never mistake one for the other. Kvelertak and Baroness throw pop hooks; Gorguts have more in common with Scott Walker than with Metallica. Cauldron and Hammers of Misfortune geek out on '80s power chords; Grave Miasma and Nile flirt with Middle Eastern modalities. Corsair is obstinately pretty; Incantation is ugly as sin.

Metal doesn't sound evil. Evil has no particular sound. Metal doesn't sound fascist—the camp commandant listening to Beethoven in the evenings has become a cliché. If you read about metal, you'll learn that it often employs Aeolian progressions, staccato rhythmic figures, perfect fifth intervals, and other things I but dimly apprehend. What metal sounds like is the biggest rock and roll you've ever heard. I have the TV on as I write this, and I'm half watching the cheesy post-apocalyptic drama *Revolution*, in which the world has gone dark, when a scene catches my attention. A band in a bar is playing Ozzy Osbourne's "Crazy Train" as if it were a My Morning Jacket song. The bartender is telling a story about the day the power came back on unexpectedly for a few minutes after fifteen years of candlelight: "That Wurlitzer over there roars to life, plays 'Ramble On' for like four whole minutes, and then just goes dark. People cried. They said it was like hearing the voice of God."* It is, of course, the voice of a god, Apollo, that issues the imperative from Rilke's stone.†

Somehow this wouldn't work as well with "Gimme Shelter" or "Born to Run." Greil Marcus wrote that Zeppelin's music "meant to

---

* The scene also demonstrates an important difference between a popular art and an elite one like poetry: the possibilities each offers for communal or collective experience differ in kind and degree. Neither the bartender nor I need to identify "Ramble On" as a Led Zeppelin song—part of the point is everybody knows this. At least in America, there is no recent poem everyone in a bar would recognize.

† Another of Sloterdijk's paraphrases of this imperative: "Seize the chance to train with a god!" He also offers an intriguing defense of the popular tendency, which I follow in this essay, to divorce the closing lines of Rilke's sonnet from their context.

storm Heaven, and it came close."[28] That's a definition of metal I can live with, or at least of metal at its best: Death's *Sound of Perseverance*, Converge's *Jane Doe*, Mercyful Fate's *Don't Break the Oath*, Mastodon's *Remission*, AC/DC's *Highway to Hell*, Van Halen's *1984*, Atheist's *Unquestionable Presence*, the last two-and-a-half minutes of Black Sabbath's "Heaven and Hell," when Terry Butler's throbbing bassline doubles in tempo and Tony Iommi solos in blizzards of single notes and Ronnie James Dio sings about the lies of this world like he's running along a collapsing bridge, one step ahead of the crevasse. They mean to storm heaven. They come close. "Go, and speed," Chaos tells Satan in *Paradise Lost*, "havoc, and spoil, and ruin are my gain."

* * *

Rock and roll says: why don't you take a good look at yourself and describe what you see—and baby, baby, baby, do you like it? It says you must change your life. But rock and roll, like all art, lies. *Publishers Weekly* closed a review of Edward Snow's translation of Rilke with the claim that "readers will be helpless, after passing through this book, against the command that closes 'Archaic Torso.'"[29] But *no one* has ever changed his life because of a poem or song. Changing your life is for Simone Weil or the Buddha. The rest of us need German poetry and Norwegian black metal because they provide the illusion that we are changing, or have changed, or will change, or even *want* to change our lives.

This is one of many points at which punk and metal dovetail.*

---

* When I interviewed Jonah Falco, drummer for the Toronto hardcore band Fucked Up (currently the planet's best band), he told me that "punk and metal have been these parallel yet constant diverging paths." They seem to me even closer, in spirit and sound, than that paradoxical metaphor implies. As guitarist Mike Haliechuk said during the same interview: "I think I just like loud music."

I just picked up my old copy of Greil Marcus's *Lipstick Traces* (a reading of punk in the light of Dada, Adorno, Lettrism, and the Situationist International) to see if Marcus might have used Rilke's lines, only to find them quoted on the inside cover, in Robert Walsh's blurb. "Destroy your safe and happy lives before it is too late" (the Mekons) is the punk version. No one ever has. The Mekons know this, just as the grindcore band Liberteer doesn't expect anyone to actually enact lyrical exhortations like "To be happy, god damn it, kill those who own property."

A pop song—and metal, for all its *fuck no*, is pop music—is a commodity, and its market conditions are written into its chord structure. It is caught up entirely in capitalism's circuits. A wash of guitars and a blast beat do not have the power to resist the contradictions they expose and express.

Imagine if, "after passing through [a] book," presto, we were "helpless" to avoid changing our lives. Sometimes I wonder what metal would sound like after capitalism, or whether we would even need metal then. I wonder the same about poetry.

* * *

The finest of the first generation of rock critics—Marcus, Christgau, Robert Palmer, Ellen Willis—ignored metal almost entirely. (Willis raved about Black Sabbath's *Vol. 4*, but only after claiming that the first three albums "are mostly awful," which is blasphemous.[30]) Their hostility makes a rough sense. These were people who grew up on Elvis and Chuck Berry, had their brains rewired by Beatles-Stones-Dylan, were on the scene for punk, and were young and smart enough to write terrific things about it. They had to make the case that rock and roll was worth writing intelligently—even intellectually—about. William Shawn had to be persuaded that popular music was something the *New Yorker* needed to cover, and that a young woman who had written for *Cheetah* magazine was the one to cover it. These critics weren't about to squander their hard-earned cultural capital on an avowedly anti-intellectual genre known primarily for its cartoon demonology. I mean, the *Ramones* were too dumb for Marcus.

This critical negligence means that metal has had the freedom to develop from its bluesy origins in England's working class into one of the most vibrantly imaginative and complex genres of popular art without a lot of outside interference or notice. (This has changed relatively recently—Ben Ratliff, for instance, writes about death metal and black metal for the *New York Times*; the metal faithful predictably cry hipster incursion.) I invite anyone who has dismissed metal from afar to check out Gorguts' *Colored Sands* and Deafheaven's *Sunbather*, two recently celebrated releases. I doubt they're what you're expecting.

I don't promise you'll like them, though. Kant claims that aesthetic judgments contain an implicit *ought*—I feel that a person ought to agree with my judgment of the beautiful, even though I recognize he may, foolishly, dissent from it. This is not how I feel about metal. I can understand why a person would not care to devote much time to music that involves a lunatic growling "Colon, cry for me!" over an unremitting tornado of guitars and drums (not that you can really make out *what* Lord Worm is growling about in Cryptopsy's "Slit Your Guts").

But I do think it's a shame to spend your middle years listening to the same old Game Theory records. The summer I was twenty-two, stumbling around Europe, I listened to the Stones' *Exile on Main St* on my Walkman at least once a day. Those songs slide right off me now. They gave me everything they had in them, and I'm grateful.

I didn't get into metal until I was in my thirties, and then only because—this is really embarrassing to admit, but as they say in AA, we're only as sick as our secrets—I was flipping through one of Robert Christgau's old *Consumer Guide* collections and saw that he'd given Slayer's *Reign in Blood* a B+. Every time I think I've got a handle on it, I turn up some unsuspected star chart that leads me off in search of ever more distant constellations. It's like being seventeen again, perusing the testimony of Christgau and Marcus, scouring every record store in town for some out-of-print Adverts' album I just had to hear.

Except, of course, it's not like being seventeen at all. That out-of-print record is a Google search away, and music can't ever again be as important to me as it was when I was young. Emerson wrote that "After thirty a man wakes up sad every morning excepting perhaps five or six until the day of his death." This is—how shall I put it—true. Listening to most rock and roll now involves remembering what it used to do for me that it can't anymore.

Recently I took my writing students to see Converge at the Metro in Chicago. It wasn't like seeing Sonic Youth in Denver in 1990. For one thing, I was in the balcony rather than pressed up against the stage like a pilgrim on the hajj. For another, I had to keep my eye on a bunch of college kids to make sure they weren't drinking alcohol on school time. But Converge (who aren't much younger than I) took over that space like a bellowing woolly rhino crashing into a Pleistocene clearing. The enormousness of that sound, its rooms and crevices. The nearest objective correlative I know is in Christopher Logue's *All Day Permanent Red,* which takes as its subject battle scenes from the *Iliad*:

> Think of a raked sky-wide Venetian blind.
> Add the receding traction of its slats
> Of its slats of its slats as a hand draws it up.
> Hear the Greek army getting to its feet.

It's war music.

At one point the band lurched into a slow, martial burner I recognized from the new record, which I was still getting to know. I listened to it again when I got home—"Empty on the Inside" (as opposed to being empty on, like, the outside?). The studio version is good, but the song had been something else onstage—feral and free, the reverberation of decreation. I googled the lyrics. And was reminded that the frequent indecipherability of Jacob Bannon's vocals is a blessing. One line struck me, though. You can barely hear it— Bannon's not singing, just kind of muttering to himself, a pervert on a park bench watching girls walk home from school.

"I can't shake these beasts from my bones."

RHYME IS A DRUG

Mongol hordes carried rhyme from China to Persia, whence mystery cults infected Rome. Or else rhyme, being a natural linguistic structure, has no particular origin, but develops spontaneously in languages with the right features. On the one hand, *The Princeton Encyclopedia of Poetry & Poetics* informs us that "it is a thundering fact that most of the world's 4,000 languages lack or avoid rhyme in their poetries altogether." On the other, "rhyme-like structures apparently exist even in nonhuman languages, such as that of whales."[31]

Since Chaucer consolidated end rhyme in English, there have been grumblers. The locus classicus of opposition, quoted by everyone who writes on the subject, is the prefatory note to *Paradise Lost*. Upon being asked by the printer of the second edition to supply "a reason of that which stumbled many others, why the Poem Rimes not," Milton wrote:

> The Measure is *English* Heroic Verse without Rime, as that of *Homer* in Greek, and *Virgil* in Latin; Rhime being no necessary Adjunct or true Ornament of Poem or good Verse, in longer Works especially, but the Invention of a barbarous Age, to set off wretched matter and lame Meeter; grac't indeed since by the use of some famous modern Poets, carried away by Custom, but much to thir own vexation, hindrance, and constraint to express many things otherwise, and for the most part worse then else they would have exprest them. Not without cause

therefore some both *Italian*, and *Spanish* Poets of prime note have rejected Rhime both in longer and shorter Works, as have also long since our best *English* Tragedies, as a thing of itself, to all judicious ears, triveal, and of no true musical delight; which consists onely in apt Numbers, fit quantity of Syllables, and the sense variously drawn out from one Verse into another, not in the jingling sound of like endings, a fault avoyded by the learned Ancients both in Poetry and all good Oratory. This neglect then of Rhime so little is to be taken for a defect, though it may seem so perhaps to vulgar Readers, that it rather is to be esteem'd an example set, the first in *English*, of ancient liberty recover'd to heroic Poem from the troublesom and modern bondage of Rimeing.

No one is likely today to suggest that poets should not rhyme because Homer and Virgil didn't (in fact both do, on rare occasion). And Hugh Kenner inserted a sly footnote at "grac't indeed since by the use of some famous modern Poets": "E.g., the author of *Lycidas*."[32]

Milton echoes the Renaissance fit against rhyme. In the late sixteenth century, Roger Ascham deplored "our rude beggarly rhyming, brought first into Italy by Goths and Huns, when all good verse and good learning too were destroyed by them, and after carried into France and Germany, and at last received into England by men of excellent wit indeed, but of small learning and less judgment in that behalf."

Various literary movements in Europe had argued that their vernacular poetries of like endings would be better off imitating the quantitative verse of the Greeks and Romans, since rhyme was a Hunnish vestige of the Dark Ages. Spenser, Campion, and Jonson inveighed against the practice, somewhat ridiculously—unlike Milton, they would scarcely be remembered if they hadn't been so good at rhyming. By the early nineteenth century, the classics envy had mostly dropped away—Blake approvingly lifts Milton's "modern bondage of Rhyming" for the preface to *Jerusalem* but fails to mention Homer or Virgil. For Whitman, "the truest and greatest Poetry . . . can never again, in the English language, be expressed in arbitrary and rhyming meter." Emerson said of Poe, "O, you mean the jingle man!" To which Ernest Fenollosa, thanks to Pound, retorted: "It is absurd to belittle this sound beauty in poetry, as to undervalue color beauty in painting" (little did he know).[33]

According to the potted histories of modernism, rhyme disappears from poetry sometime in early winter 1910, when of course it just becomes less common, along with human character. Gillian White, for instance, advises us that "for early modernism, 'rhyme' is a moribund nineteenth-century, paternalistic attachment inhibiting more authentic artistic (and truly American, modern) urges and expressions."[34] The conceptual prankster Kenneth Goldsmith has actually said that "there are no rhymes in modernism." Right. Except for those of Yeats, Frost, Eliot, Moore, Stevens, Pound, Rilke, Stein, Valéry, Williams, Zukofsky, Bunting, Mayakovsky, and a dozen others. The next two generations include such rhymers in English as Auden, Berryman, Thomas, Bishop, Lowell, Larkin, Plath, Roethke . . .

Rhyme punctuates rhythm and pleases the ear. Yet I have met several poets who have internalized the received view and seem bewildered that such a reactionary formal element should persist in our enlightened age. And yet nearly everyone who holds the modern prejudice against rhyming poetry loves the art of rhyming—who objects to Lil Wayne or the Beatles on the grounds that they *rhyme* too much? Assorted misconceptions about rhyme lead many readers to disdain its use in verse, while their love of music that rhymes is rooted in organic experience. As the poet Anthony Madrid, whose unpublished dissertation is the best thing written on the subject of rhyme in decades, put it in a hyperbolic text message to me:

> *They know damn well they like rhyme, but it's illegal to like it, according to their stupid fucking theory about it. They blame rhyme for what they perceive as the dryness/unpalatability/*

offputtingness of old poetry. When they don't like something that rhymes, they think it's because it rhymes that they don't like it.

Not, of course, that any old rhymes will do. No one mourns, for instance, the eminently mortal Thomas Holley Chivers:

> As the churches, with their whiteness,
> Clothe the earth, with her uprightness
> Clothed she now his soul with brightness,
>   Breathing out her heart's love-lore;
> For her lily-limbs so tender,
> Like the moon in her own splendor
> Seemed all earthly things to render
>   Bright as Eden was of yore.

Note, though, that what's inept in such lines aren't the rhymes themselves. A common misapprehension is that rhyme pairs like *whiteness | brightness* must be opposed on the grounds that they have been used too often before, or that they're just too simple. Pope's censure in *An Essay on Criticism* gets trotted out:

> While they ring round the same unvary'd Chimes,
> With sure Returns of still expected Rhymes.
> Where-e'er you find the cooling Western Breeze,
> In the next Line, it whispers thro' the Trees.

The facile reading has it that Pope finds the pairing of *breeze* and *trees* objectionable *in itself*—a strange position for a poet who elsewhere, more than once, rhymes *breeze* with *trees*. I was delighted to learn that Madrid had not read Kenner's "Rhyme: An Unfinished Monograph," as that means the two critics arrived independently at (almost) the same interpretation of Pope's lines. In Madrid's words, Pope is "not explicitly stating that clichéd rhymes exist and should be shunned":

Pope does not say that wherever the poet ends his line with *breeze*, you can be sure the next will end with *trees*. Instead, he mimics a poet being trapped (as it were) into generating poetic tinsel on account of the poet's not resisting the magnetism of the conventional and obvious relationship between trees and breezes. Yet there are, after all, many possible relations between those two physical realities (including no relation at all).

"I would suggest," he concludes, "that it is more likely the rhymes are 'expected' because of the phrases leading up to them, rather than because of the nature of the rhyme pair" itself.[35]

Kenner concurs, noting that Pope rhymed *breeze* with *trees* in his "Winter" pastoral (also, Madrid remarks, in *An Essay on Man* and "Eloisa to Abelard"): "Her fate is whisper'd by the gentle Breeze, / And told in sighs to all the trembling Trees." "Anyone whom the *Essay on Criticism* prompts to look back at the lines in *Winter*," Kenner continues,

> may admire Pope's skill in forfending (for fit readers) any supposition that writing *breeze* was what prompted the thought of *trees*. Pope's trees have better reasons for being there. They are sponsored by the fact that the young lady whose name they bear is named Daphne, after Ovid's nymph who became a laurel, and they tremble less at the breeze's agitation than at the news it bears, of a relative's namesake's fate. The poets Pope castigates in the *Essay* have not this ingenious energy, this mastery of superintending coherence. They write *trees* because a moment ago they wrote *breeze*, and their minds are suggestible, not capacious.

Pope's mind is not suggestible. "He means us," Kenner says, "when we are reading lines of his, to be visited by no suspicion that the first rhyme of a pair has suggested the second, or even vice versa; to judge rather that the rhyme validates a structure of meaning which other orders of cogency have produced."[36]

Chivers's lines fail because of *how* they rhyme, not *what* they rhyme, *brightness* validating only the need for a rhyme with *whiteness*. Compare the natural, robust coherence of Frost's early poem "Going for Water":

> We ran as if to meet the moon
>   That slowly dawned behind the trees,
> The barren boughs without the leaves,
>   Without the birds, without the breeze.

The conventional, expected relation of trees to breezes is adroitly sidestepped. Something has been *understood* about rhyme here, about the stillness of the evening, about how the two orders—sound and stillness, harmony and absence—might be related.

So much for the opposition to what Kenner calls "normal" rhymes, those rhyme words whose pairing we have encountered before. There exists an equally obtuse and not unrelated disdain for "simple" rhymes, rhymes that lack the ingenuity and flair of, say, Byron's *intellectual | henpecked you all*, Paul Muldoon's *zarf | scairbh*, or Clipse's *confusin' 'em | Peruvian*. Rhymes such as *change | strange*, *might | sight*, *old | told*. I hesitate even to address this "objection that only a fool would raise," as a fellow poet put it to me, but poetry is rife with fools. One of the legion of anonymous online ankle-biters scoffed at this rhyme in my poem "Country Music" when it first appeared in the *New Yorker*:

> West Point to the south of me,
> Memphis to the north.
> In between is planted with
> pinwheels for the Fourth.

A rhyme like *north | fourth* evinces no Byronic derring-do; it must be for simpletons. This is like believing that the chord progression

D-C-G is necessarily inferior to more elaborate progressions, so that just about any Genesis or Yes song is better than "Sweet Home Alabama" or "Sweet Child o' Mine."

Originality, fetish object of the young and naïve, is no virtue in itself. If it were, every free jazz collective, no matter how inept, would be superior to the Rolling Stones. What matters, again, is what you do with the rhyme, not the rhyme itself. The poet and translator Alicia Stallings is exquisitely right: "There are no tired rhymes. There are no forbidden rhymes. Rhymes are not predictable unless lines are. Death and breath, womb and tomb, love and of, moon, June, spoon, all still have great poems ahead of them."[37]

That anyone should think otherwise is probably the result of embarrassment. Centuries of jeering at jingles have produced a kind of shame at finding pleasure in rhyme—everyone is always trying to come up with some sophisticated *theory* of rhyme. In his essay "Why Rhyme Pleases," Simon Jarvis provides a catalog of calumnies directed at rhyme: "Rhyme is an idol, it is witchcraft, it is contemptible, it is depraved, it is a prostitute, it is a mercenary, it is a barbarian, it is stupefaction."[38]

Well, and what if it be witchcraft? Taking his cue from Coleridge on meter's "medicated atmosphere," Madrid argues that rhyme pleases because it acts as a kind of drug. No one is surprised that drugs please people; that's what they're for. They make you feel good, for no logical reason beyond their innate power. Madrid holds that rhyme's "seductive effect is partly secured by the reader's intuition of a poetic mandate that seems to issue from the English language itself": disparate words "are found utterly to belong together as if by the hand of some unknown, riddling divine force." Rhyme words possess "a kind of occult affinity." "Rhyme is a good thing," Madrid proposes, "precisely because it makes no logical sense."[39]

Now, as it happens, this thesis puts Madrid at odds with many of rhyme's advocates. For isn't this the most obscurantist, romantic nonsense? Is it not a touch, erm, anti-intellectual? We must have firm principles—preferably diagrammatical—on which to base our approbation of the sound of like endings. To hear *The Princeton Encyclopedia of Poetry & Poetics* tell it:

> it is essential that the definition [of rhyme] not be framed solely in terms of sound, for that would exclude the cognitive function . . . the phonic semblance (and difference) then points up semantic semblance or difference: the equivalence of the rhyme syllables or words on the phonic level implies a relation or likeness or difference on the semantic level.[40]

That is to say, rhyme is a good thing precisely because it *does* make logical sense. The affinity of rhymes is anything but occult, for it is not only sonic. One must take account of the *meanings* of the rhyme words. This is what René Wellek and Austin Warren call the "semantic function of rhyme."

Kenner shows how this is to work. Discovering such rhymes in Pope as *glade* | *shade*, *descends* | *ends*, *twines* | *vines*, he notes that "their senses concur, or at least grope toward one another." Vines twine in a shady glade as the sun descends and the day ends. So with Shakespeare's "Golden lads and girls all must, / As chimney-sweepers, come to dust." The necessity of mortality is writ into the language: "Everybody understands [the rhyme words'] relationship, and we ought to feel that ancestral wisdom patterned the language to underwrite their effects."[41]

But ought we to feel this, really? What ought we then to feel about the countless *unrhymed* word pairs whose senses are even more intimately linked? Were languages whose words for *must* and *dust* don't rhyme patterned by ancestral folly? Kenner implies that poets devote a great deal of thought to the semantic relation of their rhyme pairs. While I can believe that Pope was sometimes at pains to forestall the impression that one rhyme suggested another, and that Shakespeare might have considered affinity of sense along with affinity of sound, I often find that the semantic function has generally been overstated.

The thesis requires poets and readers to attend to the meanings of rhyme words, independent of syntactic context, in a way that doesn't jibe with my usual experience of writing and reading poems. W. K. Wimsatt's classic essay "One Relation of Rhyme to Reason" is chiefly concerned to posit that Pope's rhymes are more dynamic than those of other poets because his rhyme words are likelier to belong to different parts of speech (or to the same part in different functions). Yet, as Madrid points out, Wimsatt never explicitly claims that Pope consciously chose to vary his rhymes in this way—it could well be "an accidental effect of the powerful combination of Pope's choice of closed couplets and his commitment to packing those couplets with dense, discursive thought."[42] Nor does Wimsatt have much to say about the effect the practice is supposed to have. Few readers are likely to register the respective parts of speech of *alone* | *throne* or *eyes* | *rise*—unless they are writing an essay on the relation of rhyme to reason. And even assuming they *do* notice, how much pleasure or intellectual satisfaction will the fact provide?

For we have lost track somewhere of rhyme's reason—to give pleasure. It seems bizarre to have to make such an elementary point, but so it goes with moribund nineteenth-century, paternalistic attachments. What is so shameful about rhyme that we must forever be discovering every motivation for it *but* the sheer wild revel of phonetic harmony?

Grammatical index aside, Wimsatt admirably stresses the *alogical* character of rhyme—the play of chance, of difference and counterpoint, of delight in fortuitous connections. *Pace* Kenner, it is surely a happy accident that *must* rhymes with *dust*, and if meaning must come into the question, it does so secondarily. Rhyme casts a spell, circumvents the rational apparatus, charms the snake body. Blood-knowledge, D. H. Lawrence called it.

> While on the shop and street I gazed
> My body of a sudden blazed;
> And twenty minutes more or less
> It seemed, so great my happiness,
> That I was blessed and could bless.

Maybe Yeats's music doesn't possess you as it does me. Maybe you'd rather talk about how, although *happiness* and *bless* are semantically related, they belong to different parts of speech. As for me and my house, we serve the song.

* * *

Well, that's a bit de trop. It's the sort of thing I think when I've stayed up till two listening to Fleetwood Mac (I have never heard Stevie singing "Gypsy" and thought, "I'm not really in the mood for this song"). In other tempers, I'm with Simon Jarvis: "The pleasures of verse in no way represent some entirely unmediated category of 'sheer sensuous pleasure', however much they might feel like that. The notion of sheer sensuous pleasure, in the case of verbal art, is only the obverse of an inner logicism."[43]

Rhyme isn't, can't be, *only* sheer wild revel. When I start to think it is, I consider the practice of Paul Muldoon, our trickiest, most Byronic rhymester. Muldoon conceives of rhyme as nothing less than a furrow in which the self might fight free of fate.[44] The ninety rhymes deployed in the poems "Incantata" and "Yarrow," from *The Annals of Chile* (1994), are the same as those used in "The Mudroom" and "The Bangle (Slight Return)" from *Hay* (1998); "At the Sign of the Black Horse" from *Moy Sand and Gravel* (2002); and "Sillyhow Stride" from 2006's *Horse Latitudes*. These poems range in form from sestina to sonnet sequence to terza rima, but half of them, tellingly, are elegies: "Incantata" for Mary Powers; "Yarrow" for a former lover referred to as S—— and the poet's mother; "Sillyhow

Stride" for both Warren Zevon and Muldoon's sister. Thus the invocation of Powers in the first line of "Incantata"—"I thought of you tonight, *a leanbh*, lying there in your long barrow"—rhymes in both a prosodic and a thematic sense across twelve years with the ninety-fifth line of "Sillyhow Stride," which refers to Maureen Muldoon: "and couldn't think that she had sunk so low."

Steven Matthews calls this obsessive end-rhyme compulsion "a sign of repeatedly played out ending, of death writ o'er all."[45] But it is more than this; in a way, it is the opposite of this. For what Muldoon has crafted here is, first, a template of the self in time and, second, the creation of a new form; and these are simply different ways of saying the same thing. This method of poem assemblage—this addiction to rhyme—encodes a theory of the self, as structures persist across time through repetition with variation. The scale of the poems allegorizes the scale of a human life, as formal structures are subverted from within by discordant elements like the off rhymes that link "brim" and "pram" from "At the Sign of the Black Horse" to "barm" and "prom" in "Sillyhow Stride." Occasional lines in the poems seem to acknowledge the project; Muldoon writes in "At the Sign" of "An overwhelming sense of déjà vu." But what reader's response would even get as far as déjà vu (or déjà lu)? How likely is even the most devoted reader to notice such an arrangement? As Clair Wills says, "This is a repetitive device beyond anything which an attentive reader of the individual poem could be expected to grasp."[46]

MacDonald P. Jackson has discovered a similar structure on a smaller scale within Shakespeare's Sonnets 131 to 146, where a rhyme word in one sonnet repeats in the next, a new rhyme word from that sonnet repeats in the following sonnet, and so on.[47] Dylan Thomas's chiastic "Prologue" is another close analogue: two verse paragraphs of fifty-one lines each, with no rhymes until the fifty-first line, which rhymes with the fifty-second, the fifty-third with the fiftieth, and so on until the 102nd line rhymes backward with the first line. Here are the middle six lines:

Molten and mountainous to stream
Over the wound asleep
Sheep white hollow farms

To Wales in my arms.
Hoo, there, in castle keep,
You king singsong owls, who moonbeam

How many lines in to the second verse paragraph can any reader get before the rhymes become inaudible? If you can't hear a rhyme because one hundred lines separate one word of the pair from the other, is it still a rhyme? How about when one line appears in one poem in a book published in 1994 ("and how resolutely you would pooh-pooh") and its rhyme in another poem in a book published in 2006 ("for Diet, yeah right, *Diet* Mountain Dew")?*

If this is rhyme—if rhymes can resound across such distances— it has little to do with druggy revels. Muldoon's batty allusiveness doesn't seem meant to be "got." It frees the idea of causality from the requirements of discovery.† Given this private dimension, the project remains deeply autobiographical. Muldoon's obsessive continuation of a single rhyme scheme across several books and years is a way of grappling with death and loss of self, precisely by insisting upon the perseverance of the I, subtly undermining the poem's senses of

---

* George Puttenham's *The Arte of English Poesie* has a confusing discussion of how many "distances" may fall between rhymes; Charles F. Richardson claims that "the English ear does not carry rhymes more than three lines apart."

† A reversal of Nicholas Abraham and Mária Török's liberation of discovery from conventional notions of causal structure in *The Wolf Man's Magic Word: A Cryptonymy* (Minneapolis: University of Minnesota Press, 1986). I argue this case more fully in "Paul Muldoon's Covert Operations."

ending by inflecting the endings of his lines with obstinate continuity: *I persist, I persist.*

But it is also the creation of a form—call it the *muldoon*—that anyone might take up, an empty vessel that might be filled with any content whatsoever as long as the rhymes remain the same. For Muldoon to fill this form is to produce his own life, but its very attenuation, its possibility of infinite extension, produces a version of himself that could be carried on by anyone. In this way his self might persist as form but not content, as structure but not signification—just as we say the father lives on in the son.

This possibility is figured in "At the Sign of the Black Horse," where Muldoon writes that in the flooded aftermath of Hurricane Floyd he and his family might "climb the hill and escape . . . to a place where the soul might indeed recover / radical innocence." The latter phrase is lifted from Yeats's "A Prayer for My Daughter," and "At the Sign" is Muldoon's prayer for his son, as he signals further by appropriating the earlier poem's rhyme scheme. Walking "because of the great gloom that is in my mind," as the wind screams "in the elms above the flooded stream," and "Considering that, all hatred driven hence, / The soul recovers radical innocence, / And learns at last that it is self-delighting," Yeats imagines his daughter might some day find the happiness that has eluded him. Muldoon's poem is about his son, but on a crypt level[48] it is the form he bequeaths to future poets that might recover for him radical innocence, the innocence of formal agency without the burden of responsibility for content: thou shalt remain, in midst of other woe than ours. As Yeats writes, it is "in custom and in ceremony" that innocence is born.

Not that anyone would be mad enough to try it, this strange template of the self. (I might try it myself, one of these days.) The form's survival, and Muldoon's concomitant escape into radical innocence, remains theoretical. As a practical matter, Muldoon himself toils lonely within the form, imagining a form of freedom from within the bonds of rhyme. Thus his self-mocking aside in "Silly-how Stride," in which addiction is a delusion of freedom. Channeling Donne, Muldoon remembers the day he met the rock musician Warren Zevon, whose hard living precipitated his early death from lung cancer:

> Two graves must hide, Warren, thine and mine corse
> who, on the day we met, happened
> also to meet an individual dragging a full-length cross
>
> along 42nd Street and kept mum, each earning extra
>   Brownie points
> for letting that cup pass. The alcoholic
> knows that to enter in these bonds
>
> is to be free, yeah right.

The sense of weary resignation is only reinforced by consideration that "to enter in these bonds is to be free" is Donne's near-blasphemous (hence its occurring to Muldoon in connection with the memory of a man dragging a cross) attempt to talk his mistress into having sex with him. To enter in the bonds of his byzantine and potentially infinite rhyme scheme is to be free, Muldoon hopes—with the recognition that the answer to that hope might be "yeah right." For if we consult Donne's elegy further, we find a rebuke to the Yeatsian wish of "At the Sign of the Black Horse": "Here is no penance, much less innocence."

If this argument holds, the relation of rhyme it describes is one of intertextual logicism, scholarly rather than narcotic. And yet the muldoon is notable precisely because it is a deviation from standard rhyming practice. Rhymes are usually meant to be heard, as Captain Obvious once wrote.

I think we have to internalize the external opposition between rhyme's irrational drug effects and its logical function—they produce each other. Rhyme *is* alchemical, as Stallings says—"an irrational, sensual link between two words"—and *therefore* subject to an inner logicism. We always try to subjugate the irrational. We fear the atavistic remnants of cultic ritual. In the plays of Shakespeare, Ben Jonson, John Lyly, and Thomas Dekker, the witches cast their spells in rhyme, as did the actual (accused) witches Agnes Sampson and Isobel Gowdie, who wrote: "I sall goe intill ane haire / With sorrow, and sych, and meikle caire."[49]

We all-too-enlightened Westerners explain witchcraft away. But this doesn't mean rhyme has no logistic function any more than it means witchcraft is real.

You can guess what I *feel* most strongly, in my snake body and blood-knowledge. Madrid wrote to me: "For me, reading most 'explanations' of rhyme is like listening to some masterpiece of avian taxidermy lecture that the beauty of John Donne is that he was a genius at substituting trochees where you would 'expect' iambs."

As someone whose classroom lecture on meter includes pointing out that Donne's "Batter my heart" sonnet begins on an unexpected trochee, mimicking the sudden violence of the desired act, I wince. But I know what he means.

HOW TO WRITE A CHARLES SIMIC POEM

How to write a Charles Simic poem: Go to a café. Wait for something weird to happen. Record mouse activity. Repeat as necessary. (For "mouse," feel free to substitute "cat," "roach," "rat," "chicken," "donkey," etc.) Born in Belgrade, Simic immigrated to the United States in 1954. He inherited the uncanny sensibility of Kafka, Bruno Schulz, Vasko Popa, and other pale Quixotes whose chivalric romances were flyspecked bulbs illuminating empty cupboards. From the '60s through, say, the late '80s, Simic could summon a creepy malaise, made somehow creepier by his matter-of-fact tone, straightforward syntax, and plain language. Consider these lines from "Help Wanted," one of nearly four hundred poems collected in his *New and Selected Poems: 1962–2012*:

> They ask for a knife
> I come running
> They need a lamb
> I introduce myself as the lamb
> . . . .
> They require a shepherd
> For their flock of black widows

This has something of the dream logic of fable, with its detached pronouns and bureaucratic menace.

Simic is always referred to by critics as a surrealist, but it takes more than illogical goings-on and flocks of black widows to brew up surrealism. Rather, he removes the safety nets from the everyday, taking Viktor Shklovsky's concept of defamiliarization (*ostranenie*) literally:

> This strange thing must have crept
> Right out of hell.
> It resembles a bird's foot
> Worn around the cannibal's neck.

This is the beginning of a poem called "Fork" (it's followed by "Spoon," "Knife," "My Shoes," and "Stone"). It's a great poem to teach. Forget about self-expression, kid: learn to see the monster on the dinner table.

In his early poems, Simic is a carny barker, fast-talking up the grotesques with a snake-oil man's pinstriped charm. He zips around telling jokes in a faux-biblical register, as in the exquisitely titled "Concerning My Neighbors, the Hittites":

> Great are the Hittites.
> Their ears have mice and mice have holes.
> Their dogs bury themselves and leave the bones
> To guard the house. A single weed holds all their storms
> Until the spiderwebs spread over the heavens.

This has the quick spark of the best Monty Python sketches, but "Their ears have mice and mice have holes," with its associational slippage, is great poetry.

Selected Early Poems (first published in 1985; updated 2000), from which the first ninety pages of *New and Selected Poems* are drawn, is full of such little astonishments. The poems strut with confidence and verve. *Unending Blues* (1986), the prose poems of *The World Doesn't End* (1989), and some of the pieces in *The Book of Gods and Devils* (1990) are similarly charged.

But then Simic just stopped. I don't mean he stopped writing—he churns out books like Trollope on NoDoz. He stopped taking pains with his poems. "Many other strange things came to pass," he writes in 1990's "Factory." I sat in the coffee shop. Many other strange things came to pass. Something about flies and ashtrays. You write the poem.

It's not that he's forgotten how to make poems—he retains a mechanical efficiency, with tidy stanzas leading to some tweaked lyrical summation. But the fire's gone out of them. They're comfortable, unassuming, the sort of thing an investment banker might discover in the *New Yorker* and send to his son at MIT. A typical poem ends:

> In Los Angeles, one Sunday morning,
> The photographer took a picture
> Of a closed barbershop
> And a black cat crossing an empty avenue,
>
> A blind man outside a bus station
> Playing the guitar and singing

If the worst are full of passionate intensity, Simic would seem to be in the clear. Most of the later poems are like this, banal snapshots bewildering in their literality. Here's the last stanza of "The Melon":

> I remember a hornet, too, that flew in
> Through the open window
> Mad to taste the sweet fruit
> While we ducked and screamed,
> Covered our heads and faces,
> And sat laughing after it was gone.

If he wrote "Fork" today, it would end, "Its shiny tines reflect the light."

There is, of course, a tradition of fine poetry that distrusts metaphor. But such poetry distinguishes itself by the artfulness of its selection and articulation. Simic no longer bothers to tweak a cliché until it seems sinister: "a Vietnam vet on crutches / . . . tries to bum a dime or a cigarette." If I were commenting on a student's draft, I'd jot, "A dime or a cigarette is what you expect to follow 'bum'; what if he tried to bum something more startling?" But Charles Simic is a former poet laureate and recipient of the Pulitzer Prize.

There are moments in late Simic when the old headless chicken rears its bloody hackle: "When you play chess alone it's always your move." But as long as *Selected Early Poems*—my favorite of which, "Psalm" ("I'm Joseph of the Joseph of the Joseph who rode on a donkey"), is not included in this latest collection—and *The World Doesn't End* are in print, this edition is superfluous. In the late '90s an interviewer asked Simic where he finds inspiration. "Piece of cake," he responded. Alas.

KILL ROCK STARS' MEMOIRS

The rock-star memoir is one of those dicey genres whose success depends on exceeding the lowest possible expectations. Patti Smith's *Just Kids* was highly acclaimed despite her apparent belief that serious writing is principally a matter of avoiding contractions. Keith Richards's *Life* was *New Yorker* poetry editor Paul Muldoon's choice for book of the year despite being called *Life*. Jay Z's remarkable *Decoded* was cowritten with Dream Hampton, so it doesn't count. The gold standard is Bob Dylan's *Chronicles, Volume One* (2004), a work of freaky genius that nevertheless contains several phrases on the order of "Sigmund Freud, the king of the subconscious."

Expectations duly lowered, I was ready to give Neil Young's memoir a chance even though it is a) titled *Waging Heavy Peace* and b) written by Neil Young, who has always struggled with lyrics—you know, the writing words part. "That perfect feeling when time just slips / Away between us on our foggy trip," anyone?

Now, Neil Young is a colossus. He's reshaped rock and roll. That maelstrom of guitar fuzz you hear in Dinosaur Jr., Sonic Youth, Built to Spill, Nirvana, or in metal bands like Horseback and Royal Thunder—Neil Young made that possible. *After the Gold Rush, On the Beach, Tonight's the Night, Decade, Rust Never Sleeps*—these are sacred documents.

But as sure as this old world keeps spinning round, the man cannot write a book.

Waging Heavy Peace (it helps if you mentally substitute a better title—which is to say, any other title—whenever you read those words) is as messy as the druggiest Crazy Horse solo. Unlike a Crazy Horse record, though, there's no discernible structure, just a free-associating ramble through the haze of Young's green mind. That could be fun enough, and the old man sure has some tales to tell. But the prose. Reader, the prose.

The pull quote on the dust jacket had me worried before I'd even turned to the first page:

> I think I will have to use my time wisely and keep my thoughts straight if I am to succeed and deliver the cargo I so carefully have carried thus far to the outer reaches. Not that it's my only job or task. I have others, too. Sacred things that I need to protect from pain and hardship, like careless remarks on an open mind.

Ah, the weird Victorian transmissions of the amateur writer. Who says "I so carefully have carried thus far"? Why both "job" and "task"? What does the last clause modify? What could it mean for a "careless remark" to be "on" an "open mind"?

Indeed, there is not a hint of inspiration on any page of *Waging Heavy Peace*, nothing to indicate Young has any idea that sentences can do more than impart basic information:

> There is a lot of misinformation about ethanol. . . . The production of the concert got some awards as well and was seen as bold at the least. That made [the producer David] Briggs and me feel pretty good. The movie we made of the concert is one of my favorites. . . . I got a few sexually transmitted diseases and started to become aware that there was a responsibility connected to the decisions I was making. . . . We had some really great times, David and I! That was only one of them! I am laughing my ass off right now just thinking of the fun we had! How lighthearted.

No one expects belles lettres from rock stars, but it's depressing to learn that one of your heroes writes like a composition student aiming for the earnest tone of a public service announcement. Without a wink of irony, Young will exclaim "That's life!" or end a chapter with "The sky was the limit." Compare Dylan in *Chronicles*:

> Once when I was lying on the beach in Coney Island, I saw a portable radio in the sand . . . a beautiful General Electric, self-charging—built like a battleship—and it was broken. . . . I had seen a lot of other things broken, too—bowls, brass lamps, vessels and jars and jugs, buildings, buses, sidewalks, trees, landscapes—all these things, when they're broken, make you feel ill at ease.

This is mysterious, haunting in a way that's reminiscent of Dylan's best songs, even though he's describing one of his worst ("Everything Is Broken"). It's not a coincidence that Dylan spends pages hyperventilating over Rimbaud and Byron and Faulkner and Coleridge, while the only indication in *Waging Heavy Peace* that Neil Young has ever read a single book comes when he mentions buying a used Clive Cussler novel.

Soft target, you say? Well, the guy did write a book, and he is asking you to throw thirty of your clams at it. But all right, what about the content? Turns out it's the extension of form. Young is never more frustrating than when he finally threatens to get to the good stuff. "It's better to burn out than to fade away" serves as the epigraph to a chapter that begins by noting that line's relationship to both John Lennon and Kurt Cobain. But Young has little to say about Lennon or Cobain. The chapter devolves into a mash note to Jimmy Fallon.

Playing guitar with Charlie Manson merits a couple of perfunctory paragraphs. After Hurricane Katrina, Neil gets a call from his "old friend Bruce." It's Bruce Springsteen! On the phone with Neil Young! What did they talk about! Who knows! "There is no need to go into what two old friends had to say to each other at this point." Right. Unless you're trying to write an interesting book.

Instead, if you read *Waging Heavy Peace*, you will learn more than you ever wanted to know about model trains and old cars, Young's obsessive hobbies. You will thrill to PowerPointillist descriptions of his business meetings. You will be told that all good things must pass, but no one knows why. You will be made to feel guilty about listening to MP3s. You will wonder just how many sentences in a single memoir can begin "Anyway . . ." You will marvel at the astonishments of the LincVolt. (I think this is a kind of electric car, but it is so boring to read about that I learned to start skimming whenever the word *LincVolt* loomed in my peripheral vision.)

And you will find it affecting to listen in as this aging artist mourns his lost friends, as he worries that the cloud on his MRI presages the dementia that felled his father, as he likens his forty years of drug and alcohol use to a big sleep. The simplicity of the prose befits these moments: in a chapter devoted to heroin casualties we learn that when producer Jack Nitzsche overdosed, "I was on the road. I didn't know what else to do, so I just sent flowers."

The chapter should have ended there. But Young cannot resist what Greil Marcus once called the "traditional Neil Young sappiness," so we get some guff about life in full bloom and having faith when darkness falls. It's easier to forgive the sap when a galaxy-spawning guitar solo is around the bend. If you really want to wage some heavy peace, do yourself a favor and put on "Cowgirl in the Sand" or "Hey Hey, My My (Into the Black)." There's little ragged glory to be had from this open mind's careless remarks.

DARK, DARK, DARK

Dark, black, twilight, loneliness, darkening, winter, isolated, dark, ashes, loneliness, terribly, terrible, blind, weep, nothing, ashes, fear, waste, sufferings, poison, hatred, kills, dying, gray, night, dying, suicidally, terribly, black, empty, evening, darkens, wasted, dark, hatred, frightened, sorrow, shadows, death, dark, fear, killed, dark, dark, dark.

That's a compilation of keywords, in order of appearance, from the first nine poems of James Wright's 1963 collection *The Branch Will Not Break*. As you might have gathered, Wright is not the least melodramatic poet ever to bleed all over the thorns of life. In one poem from *Branch* he actually writes that his body is "crying / In its dark thorns. / Still, / There are good things in this world." Cool, keep us posted.

Wright was the first poet I fell in love with after deciding I wanted to write poetry. He was my North, my South Detroit, my small town girl. My fascination with these lines from "To the Muse" ensured I would not write a good poem for many years:

> Oh Jenny.
> I wish to God I had made this world, this scurvy
> And disastrous place. I
> Didn't, I can't bear it
> Either . . .

As a callow nineteen-year-old, I found Wright's romanticized "Jenny" a portable signifier, more approachable than Petrarch's Laura or Dante's Beatrice. She was Sarah Chesnutt, the combat-booted goddess of my college workshops. (We're friends on Facebook now. She's married, has a kid. Hi, Sarah.) Jenny was everyone who ever left "the scars / Of forgotten swans" incused upon my heart.

Robert Hass (another early influence, about whom more anon) has said that "the suffering of other people" becomes, in Wright's poems, "part of his own emotional life."[50] This is clearly what the poems aim for, but not always what they achieve. It is often truer to say that the suffering of other people becomes a proxy for Wright's own suffering. Other people seem to matter for him, at his worst, only insofar as they provide structural equivalents of his own "loneliness" and "anguish" and other such interchangeable markers of the utter desolation that is his:

> The cracked song
> Of my own body limps into the body
> Of this living place. I have nobody
> To go in with
> But my love who is a woman,
> And my crude dead, my sea . . .

It is easy to feel that, if fetal alcohol syndrome could write poetry, it would write this poetry. Or consider this passage from "Many of Our Waters: Variations on a Poem by a Black Child":

> I feel lonesome,
> And sick at heart,
> Frightened,
> And I don't know
> Why.
> *help.*

This is *literally* the sort of thing you might find in a high school student's journal. Presumably that's why the next lines are "The kind of poetry I want to write is / The poetry of a grown man." But do those lines justify Wright's having written the poetry of a tween?

When I was young, Wright's emotionally freighted repetition seemed talismanic, as if he were holding off the dark by naming it over and over. I tried it, mouthing "dark" and "darkness" and "darkening" as I wrote my idiotic dirges. (I just made that up, but it sounds like the kind of thing I would have done.) Any fetish, though, loses its virtue through overuse. How much more powerful than anything in Wright are Whitman's sympathy and restrained expression:

> It is not upon you alone the dark patches fall,
> The dark threw its patches down upon me also,
> The best I had done seemed to me blank and suspicious,
> My great thoughts, as I supposed them, were they not in
>   reality meagre?

I had to destroy James Wright, like Journey and Dylan Thomas, in order to save myself. They were always wrong, the old masters. When you're young you either shatter your idols or they consume you. Only now, having reached the heretofore unthinkable age of forty, do I begin to see that we never really kill our fathers. Harold Bloom, in his mad, brilliant *Anxiety of Influence*, writes that "the later poet opens himself to what he believes to be a power in the parent-poem that does not belong to the parent proper, but to a range of being just beyond that precursor."[51]

But in Wright's best work, such as the second of the "Two Poems about President Harding," a power pulses that is not his alone, and therefore not soaked in the ethanol of the self:

> A hundred slag piles north of us,
> At the mercy of the moon and rain,

> He lies in his ridiculous
> Tomb, our fellow citizen.

The poem's final lines hearken back to this opening:

> America goes on, goes on
> Laughing, and Harding was a fool.
> Even his big pretentious stone
> Lays him bare to ridicule.
> I know it. But don't look at me.
> By God, I didn't start this mess.
> Whatever moon and rain may be,
> The hearts of men are merciless.

I hear the music of Wright's beloved Thomas Hardy in this. Rather than private tokens of loneliness, the moon and rain are natural forces: symbols, to be sure, but symbols of the impersonal erosion of time, like the wind and rain that erase the names—and, metonymically, the memory of their bearers—on Hardy's headstones in "During Wind and Rain."

Except that Wright's "at the mercy of" seems to embed the possibility that the moon might harbor mercy in its heart—could not, at any rate, harbor less than humans do in theirs. This notion, along with Wright's rhyme scheme, recalls my favorite of Hardy's poems, "I Looked Up from My Writing" (unaccountably excluded from both the Faber & Faber and Oxford World's Classics editions of Hardy's selected poems):

> I looked up from my writing,
>   And gave a start to see,
> As if rapt in my inditing,
>   The moon's full gaze on me.
>
> Her meditative misty head
>   Was spectral in its air,

And I involuntarily said,
"What are you doing there?"

The moon replies that she has been "scanning pond and hole / and waterway hereabout," looking for the body of a man who drowned himself from grief at his son's death in the Great War. (Wright's Jenny is discovered, drowned perhaps, in a "suckhole.") Hardy is as pessimistic as Wright, but his sympathy seems less feigned. The poem concludes:

"Did you hear his frenzied tattle?
    It was sorrow for his son
Who is slain in brutish battle,
    Though he has injured none.

"And now I am curious to look
    Into the blinkered mind
Of one who wants to write a book
    In a world of such a kind."

Her temper overwrought me,
    And I edged to shun her view,
For I felt assured she thought me
    One who should drown him too.

I imagine the moon spitting the word *book* with contempt.

For both poets, the sense that the world is hardly fit for men to live in is connected with poetic making and with the avoidance of accusatory gazes. "Don't look at me," Wright says. "By God, I didn't start this mess." In "To the Muse," he denies having "made this world, this scurvy / And disastrous place." Hardy is shamed by the moon's looking at him (looking into his "blinkered mind") in the act of making a poem, a vocation the moon condemns as—what? trivial? useless? insensitive, inappropriate in a world of suffering? The moon summons something of the spirit of Theodor Adorno's endlessly repeated line about the barbarism of poetry-making after Auschwitz. To write a poem is, ultimately, a redemptive act, a profession of faith in beauty (whether or not the poem is "beautiful"). But in a world where sons are pointlessly slaughtered, fathers drown themselves, and the hearts of men are merciless, the promise of redemption is a bad joke and beauty an insult.

Wright's moon is less chatty, more equivocal in its quality of mercy. But in each case the moon is contrasted with a merciless human world represented by the poet "rapt in [his] inditing." This inditing the moon indicts. But Hardy, as Wright says of Harding in the first of his two poems, claims "the secret right / to be ashamed." Wright, as we have seen, explicitly disclaims responsibility for the world—he didn't start the fire.

Perhaps, however, Wright protests too much. Oren Izenberg has written that George Oppen's "Of Being Numerous" resolves "upon an *attitude toward looking*."[52] We might say that Wright's and Hardy's poems resolve upon attitudes toward *being looked at*. In addition to its idiomatic sense of "I'm not the one responsible," "Don't look at me" can mean "I'm ashamed," "I edge to shun your view." The gaze of the other, Sartre tells us, enslaves us, places us in the other's power. It's the idea behind X-Ray Specs—"see through clothes!" "Do not look upon me," says Hamlet, ashamed at his inaction, to the accusing ghost of his father.

It is strange to insist that you didn't make the world. And it's strange to wish you had made it. Such language records the disenchantment of poetic power. The entry for "Poet" in *The Princeton Encyclopedia of Poetry & Poetics* begins:

The Greeks called the poet a "maker"—*poiētēs* or *poētēs*—and that word took hold in Lat. and other Eur. langs., incl. It., Fr., and Eng. But what precisely does the poet make? The obvious answer is poems, the arrangements of words that he or she composes. Yet poets have often been given credit for bolder kinds of making. According to ancient Gr. fables, Amphion built Thebes from stones his songs called into place, and Orpheus's songs drew trees and beasts and stones to follow him. Ren. critics allegorized these stories as the harmonious beginning of civilization: poets had tamed the wilderness and softened the hearts of men. In the *Defence of Poesy*, Philip Sidney thought that the poet delivered a golden world, "in making things either better than Nature bringeth forth, or, quite anew, forms such as never were in Nature." Potentially that power of creation resembles, at one remove, the power of the Creator who first made the world.[53]

Poets no longer have such power of creation—far from softening the hearts of men, they know "the hearts of men are merciless," and they can only either wash their hands of the "mess" or feel ashamed at their powerlessness. Poems are a meager response to a scurvy and disastrous world in which hardly anyone reads them. But all that edging from view and *don't look at me* don't prevent Hardy and Wright from offering up their poems. "All I am is a poet," says Wright in the wonderfully bad "Many of Our Waters." And it would be a betrayal of his art, and Hardy's, to respond, "That's almost enough."

NO TASTE OF MY OWN

In my late teens and early twenties, my judgments of certain films were not my own, which didn't prevent me from spouting them with a no doubt ridiculous air of authority. My judgments were principally those of Pauline Kael. She was the first tastemaker I trusted implicitly. I wince to think of the times I decided I didn't really like a movie I liked because she'd dissed it, or corrected someone's approbation of a film she disdained, which as often as not I hadn't seen.

I don't think this is an uncommon phenomenon. It's related to the process Auden describes in *The Dyer's Hand*, although he doesn't mention criticism (he is doing it):

> In adolescence we realize that there are different kinds of pleasure, some of which cannot be enjoyed simultaneously, but we need help from others in defining them. Whether it be a matter of taste in food or taste in literature, the adolescent looks for a mentor in whose authority he can believe. He eats or reads what his mentor recommends and, inevitably, there are occasions when he has to deceive himself a little; he has to pretend that he enjoys olives or *War and Peace* a little more than he actually does.

The bit about olives proves Auden was English, but the rest describes my own experience. It's a kind of indoctrination, mostly benign, into canons. Auden continues:

Between the ages of twenty and forty we are engaged in the process of discovering who we are, which involves learning the difference between accidental limitations which it is our duty to outgrow and the necessary limitations of our nature beyond which we cannot trespass with impunity. Few of us can learn this without making mistakes, without trying to become a little more of a universal man than we are permitted to be. . . . When someone between twenty and forty says, apropos of a work of art, "I know what I like," he is really saying "I have no taste of my own but accept the taste of my cultural milieu," because, between twenty and forty, the surest sign that a man has a gen-uine taste of his own is that he is uncertain of it.[54]

Now, this account leaves out a good deal, most strikingly the di-mensions of class that inform one's accrual of cultural capital. Or, rather, it includes those dimensions precisely insofar as their omission is one of the surest signs that they are operating at the level of ideology. "Discov-ering who we are" makes it sound as if there is some essential, authentic self out there waiting for our embrace. (I elided Auden's caution against being led astray by ideology at this stage, since he simply means ideol-ogy that proclaims itself as such to the clear-headed bourgeois observer.)

But in its broad strokes, Auden's narrative will do. In middle age, I find I don't care about Kael's judgments. Some of her most cher-ished films—notably *Nashville* and *Last Tango in Paris*—strike me as callow, while I revere many of those she dismissed (*Céline and Julie Go Boating, All That Heaven Allows, Monkey Business*). The Library of America's selection of her writings contains no mention of two of my favorite filmmakers, Kenji Mizoguchi and Douglas Sirk, and only a passing reference to a third, Jacques Tati.* She loathed Elaine May's

---

* She praised Mizoguchi's *Ugetsu* and a couple of Tati's films, but panned the latter's wonderful *Mon Oncle*. According to Jonathan Rosenbaum, she was

uneasy rhythms; John Cassavetes's *Faces* was "dumb"; Nicholas Ray's *In a Lonely Place* is "hollow." She was frequently hostile toward Howard Hawks, the later Godard, and Robert Bresson.

These are familiar objections to Kael's work, though they're often advanced with considerable nastiness, as if they somehow invalidated her criticism.* And I suppose they do, if what you want from criticism is corroboration of your taste.

I agree more often with, for instance, Jonathan Rosenbaum. But Rosenbaum's writing, as writing, means almost nothing to me, while Kael's criticism is a permanent feature of my consciousness. It will last, because she was—to put it in terms she never shied from—a master of the medium. She could see into a film's crannies in an offhand way that was also, somehow, precision-guided. Shelley Duvall in *The Shining* "looks more like a Modigliani than ever." On *Fast Times at Ridgemont High*: "If you're eating a bowl of Rice Krispies and some of them don't pop, that's O.K., because the bowlful has a nice, poppy feeling."

Film criticism, as the youngest form of criticism, is brightly alive (at its best) to the question of what we turn to criticism *for*. (I'm not qualified to judge whether video games constitute a new art form, but they don't seem yet to have evolved a criticism worthy of the name.) The first movie was made in 1888 (or 1878 or 1889 or 1893 or 1895, depending on your definition). Maxim Gorky published a (killer) review of some films by the Lumière brothers in 1896:

---

bored by Tati's masterpiece, *Playtime*, which taught me a new way of seeing. Sirk's schmaltz turned her off.

* Michael Wolff—introducing Renata Adler, *After the Tall Timber* (New York: New York Review Books, 2015)—calls Kael a "hysteric," a "gasbag," a "bully," a "suck-up," and a "drama queen," concluding that "Kael is unread now." Since this is false, the only response—as to Adler's ridiculous claim that Kael's *When the Lights Go Down* is "line by line, worthless"—is to shrug: something's going on here, but it has zip to do with Kael's writing.

Last night I was in the Kingdom of Shadows. If you only knew how strange it is to be there. It is a world without sound, without colour. . . . Here I shall try to explain myself, lest I be suspected of madness or indulgence in symbolism. I was at Aumont's and saw Lumière's cinematograph—moving photography. The extraordinary impression it creates is so unique and complex that I doubt my ability to describe it with all its nuances. However, I shall try to convey its fundamentals. When the lights go out in the room in which Lumière's invention is shown, there suddenly appears on the screen a large grey picture. . . .

Imagine trying to explain what a movie is to someone with no concept of any aspect or appurtenance of the film medium or filmgoing experience. How would you begin to describe it—the dark, the hush, the clattering machine, then the miracle?

Criticism is parasitic literature. Everyone knows that someone said, "Writing about music is like dancing about architecture"—a pithy but fatuous credo of anti-intellectualism. It's remarkable that we're driven to write about art—to explain, judge, describe, elucidate, analyze, hate, rhapsodize, tell a story. We can't let them be—cathedrals, blockbusters, poems, pictures, statues, songs. They demand words from us.

Some aspects of film criticism, as of all criticism, go back at least to Aristotle. I imagine a goatherd sitting around a fire 2,800 years ago complaining that Homer's catalog of ships is too long, while another goatherd tries to find words to describe how what he's just heard has floored him.

Writing about music is like writing about architecture (except different). John Ruskin: "It is . . . no question of expediency or feeling whether we shall preserve the buildings of past times or not. *We have no right whatever to touch them*. They are not ours." What is ours is, for instance, "to find out how far Venetian architecture reached the universal or perfect type of Gothic, and how far it either fell short of it, or assumed foreign and independent forms."[55]

We eventually ask of a critic not "What should I think of this movie?" but "How can you unsettle my thinking about movies?" or "What can you teach me about what I don't want from them?" And we return to the critics we love for reasons that, it may be, have little to do with movies (or literature or music or architecture) and everything to do with the play of wit and insight and the construction of sentences. So it's silly of Richard Brody to write that she "was largely a first-person essayist who made use of movies to write brilliantly of the times and of herself."[56] In context, this is even more condescending than it sounds—Brody implies that Kael wasn't *really* a critic at all.

But the best criticism is always personal, and it would be truer to say that Kael made use of the times and of herself to write brilliantly about movies.

What I want from criticism is that it make me think about art in new ways, or respond to things in it I hadn't before. Kael has said all this better than I can:

> The role of the critic is to help people see what is in the work, what is in it that shouldn't be, what is not in it that could be. He is a good critic if he helps people understand more about the work than they could see for themselves; he is a great critic, if by his understanding and feeling for the work, by his passion, he can excite people so that they want to experience more of the art that is there, waiting to be seized. He is not necessarily a bad critic if he makes errors in judgment. (Infallible taste is inconceivable; what could it be measured against?) He is a bad critic if he does not awaken the curiosity, enlarge the interests and understanding of his audience. The art of the critic is to transmit his knowledge of and enthusiasm for art to others.[57]

John Jeremiah Sullivan writes of Guns N' Roses, a band I thought I knew as well as anyone else on the planet:

And what does she say, this Devil Woman [Sullivan's name for one of Axl Rose's voices]? What does she always say, for that matter? Have you ever thought about it? I hadn't. "Sweet Child," "Paradise City," "November Rain," "Patience," they all come down to codas—Axl was a poet of the dark, unresolved coda—and to what do these codas themselves come down? "Everybody needs somebody." "Don't you think that you need someone?" "I need you. Oh, I need you." "Where do we go? Where do we go now?" "I wanna go." "Oh, won't you please take me home?"[58]

No, I hadn't ever thought about it, but now I always will.

In other words, what I want from criticism is, to put it crudely, great writing, which will always involve great noticing:

She asks him what he thinks of a reproduction she is trying on the wall, and he answers, "Not bad." This doesn't show that he's sufficiently impressed and she reprimands him with, "Renoir was a very great painter." In disgust he replies, "I said 'Not bad.' " There's no doubt which of them responds more.[59]

That's Kael, on Godard's *Breathless*. And how I wish she were around to respond more.

REAL GOD, ROLL

I would begin with a word against collected editions of poetry—or at least against the current trend of issuing them in gigantic, over-priced formats that resemble the *Compact OED*. You should not be able to stun a moose with anyone's Complete Poems. In recent years, we've had enormous, expensive editions of, inter alios, Robert Lowell, Barbara Guest, Kenneth Koch, Frederick Seidel, James Merrill, Lucille Clifton, Louise Glück, Jack Gilbert, and Denise Levertov. Even so skinny a poet as Philip Larkin, in FSG's recent (and superfluous) *Complete Poems*, has bloated beyond recognition. I'm all for having these folks' oeuvres in print (although I'd also say a word against the fantasies of totality that compel editors to include drafts, revisions, juvenilia, and the like). But what's wrong with affordable and portable? The Library of America and Faber and Faber, for instance, manage to produce wieldy omnibuses (the former's, admittedly, not exactly budget-friendly). Another world is possible.

This rant was inspired by the University of South Carolina Press, whose 4.2-lb. *Complete Poems of James Dickey* will run you $85. If you have any interest in (and are not writing a dissertation or monograph on) James Dickey's poetry, may I suggest a used copy of *The Whole Motion: Collected Poems, 1945–1992*, published by Wesleyan, which lacks ninety-three poems published in the USC edition and contains many typos but has the virtues of arranging the poems by individual collection (editor Ward Briggs has printed the poems in order of initial publication) and of fitting in a messenger bag or backpack?

So much for *The Complete Poems of James Dickey*. What about the complete poems of James Dickey? Reputation is a funny thing. Dickey was once king of the cats—winner of the National Book Award (for *Buckdancer's Choice*, 1966), consultant in poetry to the Library of Congress (1966–68), author of the novel (1970) and screenplay (1972) *Deliverance* (but not of the immortal line "I bet you can squeal like a pig"). In the '60s, Peter Davison pronounced Dickey and Lowell the only major poets of their generation (Davison appears to have backed away from this; such are the hazards of cultural prophecy). In the '70s, after the success of *Deliverance*, the poet appeared on national talk shows, wrote Jimmy Carter's inaugural poem, and commemorated the Apollo missions in the pages of *Life*. In 1976, *The Paris Review* said his name was "a household word." A sense of the critical veneration to which Dickey was subject can be gleaned from Robert Kirschten's introduction to *The Selected Poems*: "I think you will agree that one would as soon read James Dickey as live."[60] Hmm, let's see . . . read Dickey; live . . . read Dickey; live . . .

It is possible that the relative dim of Dickey's star since his death is simply a reversion to sanity. But it's also, I think, an implicit recognition that his best poems, as Richard Howard implies in his brief foreword to the Briggs edition, are those collected under the title *Poems 1957–1967*, and particularly the ones published in the last few years of that decade. In the last thirty years of his career, Dickey too often gave full-throated vent to an oracular windiness. Consider these lines from "The Surround":

> Pray, beginning sleeper, and let your mind dissolve me as I
> Straighten, upright from the overflow crouch: pray with all
> Your heart-muscle,

> The longing-muscle only, as the bird in its hunting sorrows
> Bides in good falling—

Part of me wants to respond: Whose longing-muscle prays not, as the bird in its hunting sorrows bides in good falling?

But my better angel protests that the artificiality of this register is not inherently ridiculous—that its true fault lies in settling too easily for the bombastic, and it attains to a certain power even so. "Pray, beginning sleeper . . . as I / Straighten, upright from the overflow crouch" has a satisfying oddity that is undermined by the blurriness of dissolving minds and longing muscles. The trope of death as a form of sleep is shocked into life by the addition of "beginning," with its ambitious suggestion that the newly dead are initiates into cultic mysteries, with ropes to learn. "All stark soul and overreach": that's James Dickey. But you could say the same of Whitman or Dickinson, Stevens or Pound.

* * *

I fell in love with the poems of Dickey's friends James Wright and Richard Hugo at too early an age, blessedly, to hear how often they sound like the smartest drunk at the bar on any small-town afternoon. I didn't come to Dickey until after I'd been delivered by the good news John Ashbery brings to Middle-American poets manqué in their early twenties, and by then it was too late. Reading him again in my forties, I'm amused to find my prejudices both confirmed and upended. Flipping from some of the almost priggishly static early work—

> Shines, like a marsh, the sun
> On the crossed brow of listening.
> He beats his empty hands on his ears, and twists
> All around his leg, white, edged gold, sewn flat
> Beside a hooded falcon burned in grass

—to the war whoop of the last poems—

Real God, roll

roll as a result
Of a whole thing: ocean:

Thís: wide altar-shudder of miles

Given twelve new dead-level powers
Of glass, in borrowed binoculars, set into

The hand-held eyes of this man

—you get the sense someone told him he was holding the reins too
tightly and he thought, *All right, then, I'll go to hell.* The later poems
have a Poundian energy, an arrogance, that can be both daft and
charming. But they seem to want to say more than they do—they
would speak of final things in thunder but must settle for shout-
ing about next-to-last things. Howard says, "Dickey grew too big
for mere poetry," but poetry, even at its merest, is big enough for
anything James Dickey could have thrown at it. It's rather that his
poetry grew too small for its unruly grandiloquence. Even while
acknowledging, with the trope of binoculars, that his eyes are borrowed and too powerful for the scene—the Beowulf poet at the
beach—he compares his son's riding in on the surf to the Last Days
("his second son coming to his head / Like Armageddon, with the
last wave").

It's in the middle poems that Dickey flashes out into raw, free
sharpness. A real god rolls through "May Day Sermon to the Women
of Gilmer County, Georgia, by a Woman Preacher Leaving the Bap-
tist Church," a diesel-fumed negative hallelujah of backwoods terror:

Each year at this time I shall be telling you of the Lord
—Fog, gamecock, snake and neighbor—giving men all the
    help they need

> To drag their daughters into barns.
> . . . .
>   Telling: telling of Jehovah come and gone
> Down on His belly descending creek-curving blowing
> His legs
> Like candles, out putting North Georgia copper on His head

Dickey moves into the sermon form like the devil himself, flicking his forked tongue above the congregants, preaching at full throttle for ten giant pages, his voice never breaking, soaring past country girls "dancing with God in a mule's eye," "the black / Bible's white swirling ground," past an incestuous father "rambling / In Obadiah," past a needle passing "through the eye of a man bound for Heaven," past hogs and quartermoons, an old man "with an ice-pick on his mind, / A willow limb in his hand," the kudzu advancing, "its copperheads drunk and tremendous / With hiding, toward the cows."

And I would just go on quoting if I could, because Dickey finds in this poem—and in "The Christmas Towns," "For the Last Wolverine," "Adultery," and a dozen more—a canvas large enough for his palette. The closing lines of "May Day Sermon" are worth a hundred Armageddons:

>   the animals walk through
> The white breast of the Lord muttering walk with nothing
> To do but be in the spring laurel in the mist and self-sharpened
> Moon walk through the resurrected creeks through the Lord
> At their own pace the cow shuts its mouth and the Bible is still
> Still open at anything we are gone the barn wanders over the earth.

*   *   *

Dickey remained to the end a votary of that period style that liked its bourbon neat and its hawks locked in spiritual combat. "The Surround," Dickey said, is a kind of elegy for the American poet James Wright, a close friend of mine for years, who feared the change from day to night and the coming of the predators, when the whole climate of fighting in the animal world changes to that of prey and predator, in the dark: he used to say that he feared the dark because he feared the change "in the surround." I am telling him in the poem that he is not to fear this anymore, for he is the surround; the whole thing good and bad, and that the moon is beautiful on water, and that the tree grows its rings in the dark as well as the light.[61]

This is, on the one hand, sentimental trash, and, on the other, an eloquent deployment of a vocabulary in which Dickey and certain of his contemporaries were so at home that they mistook it for a kind of natural language. Robert Bly, who accused Dickey of macho warmongering, had more in common with him than he imagined.

For all their stylistic differences, these poets shared a somewhat desperate (and somewhat ridiculous) refusal to accept that the cultural authority of the Poet had been eclipsed. If I've lapsed into psychological criticism, it is because their poetry was so often nakedly psychological—a sifting of correlatives of moods and inner states. For Dickey, these were often "old-stone," deliberately archaic, as if the only horses alive enough were painted on the recesses of Altamira. Someone should count the appearances of the moon—that old bone—in Dickey's poetry. Even now he is crouched beneath it, wrapped in a bearskin and stoned on glory, trying to shape-shift into a wolf.

"

RED

On her fourth album, Nashville's twenty-two-year-old ambassador to the malls of America is feeling a bit insecure about her status: "We Are Never Ever Getting Back Together" finds her ex listening to "some indie record that's much cooler than mine"; she and her friends "dress up like hipsters" on "22" and get dissed by the "cool kids."

It's never a good idea for megastars to complain about how uncool they are, but she has a point. Aren't we finished condescending to Taylor Swift yet? If a young female songwriter this talented and consistent were making indie music on Domino Records, would critics find it necessary to congratulate her for writing her own songs or reproach her for naïve sentiments? Have these people ever *listened* to the xx? Forget Swift's age (even if she did write "Tim McGraw," the best teenage lyric since Rimbaud's "Drunken Boat," when she was a freshman in high school), her Forever-21-fresh image, her alleged ideological failings, *Red* is as smart and catchy as any album of this century. Pardon me if I hear more vitality and verve in her corniest love-story/break-up anthem than in all the adolescent morosity Justin Vernon wrings from his wounded soul.

Swift's third album, 2010's *Speak Now*, had its boggy moments (though it also had "Dear John," one of her best songs), but most of record four is on ground as firm as an endless country road in August. There are a few puddles: Taylor, if you're reading this, the slow ones *aren't working* ("featuring Gary Lightbody of Snow Patrol" is not the most promising phrase to see tagged to an MP3 file). And the vocals could be tighter and less mannered: "The trademark catch in her voice," Greil Marcus e-mailed me, "makes her the fourth, white-girl member of Destiny's Child."

But most of these songs go down like pop punch spiked by pros. The gorgeous "All Too Well" cribs the bass line from U2's "With or Without You" and dances "'round the kitchen in the refrigerator light." "Starlight" disco-dazzles Swift right out of her usual AOR persona. On "State of Grace" and "Holy Ground"—which, with their chugging rhythms and guitar filigree, sort of *are* indie rock, except without the creative writing–workshop world-wariness—Swift gets staccato over Larry Mullen–sized drums and *whoa-oh-oh-oh-whoa* cheerleader chants. And "We Are Never Ever Getting Back Together," cowritten with Max Martin, is the best hit Kelly Clarkson never had, a venomous confection of processed guitars. It's a monster. You can hear the Bubblicious smacking in Hot Topics across the land as Taylor Nation sings along.

Is it country? Country fans and country radio seem to think so.* The question usually just reveals the ignorance of its asker. Listen to Jerrod Niemann's "Free the Music," Keith Urban's "Used to the Pain," the Band Perry's "Miss You Being Gone," or Miranda Lambert's "Kerosene," then get back to me about what country music is. My answer: the most dynamically vibrant pop genre of the last decade or so. Sure, the tropes that, like the "autumn leaves" of "All Too Well," "fall down like pieces into place" are generic enough to fit any genre. On *Red*, someone has "a new Maserati," but only "dead-end streets" and "little town streets" to drive it down. Autumn's a season of mists; summers, boys pick you up on the boardwalk, you sing along with the car radio, then they stop calling.

---

* After *1989*—a record I love almost as much as *Red*—I'll take no for an answer.

It's just that country has been, for some time, the genre with the least need to be humorless about its own identity (Brad Paisley's "This Is Country Music" is *funny*). Is "All love ever does is break and burn and end" too earnest for you, even with its tail of Donnean iambs? Country's very hospitality to the unironic—Springsteen surges, Bon Jovi licks—is what gives it the scope of actual irony, dialectical and reflective: "happy, free, confused, and lonely at the same time," as Swift puts it on "22."

Whatever it is, this music is full of adult pleasures, even if the most explicit image Swift offers is of an ex-boyfriend sniffing her scarf because it smells like her. On *Red*—the color of blood and lipstick and fire and southern dirt and hearts and conservatism and tractors and communism and sin, this last a word whose charged valence here might discomfit know-it-alls who would never use it without scare quotes—Swift's too smart and tuneful to condescend to her contradictions. Or to yours.

"

MAKE THE MACHINE SING

In 1937 Sergei Eisenstein noted an affinity between filmic montage and the imagistic sequencing Homer employed in *The Iliad*. Joanna Paul, in *Film and the Classical Epic Tradition*, traces several arguments "that certain pre-modern societies understand visuality in a way that can be equated to cinema."[62] Paul Leglise, working from Lucretius's conception of vision, wrote in 1958 that "it is no paradox to claim that the new terms" of cinema "define very exactly certain literary techniques used by an ancient Latin poet."[63] Leglise thought of Virgil, not Homer, as the first cineaste; in 1970 we find Alain Malissard arguing that Homer's poetry, not Virgil's, anachronistically exemplifies the seventh art.

Obviously, it is problematic to liken ancient poetry to a medium that was invented around the same time as Coca-Cola. But I've been thinking of *The Iliad* in cinematic terms since I first read it in college, when I was also learning about Eisenstein and Alexander Dovzhenko, Godard and Nicholas Ray. Eisenstein, drawing on G. E. Lessing's *Laocoön*, isolates Homer's description of Hera's chariot, pointing out how the poet depicts the wheels in stages. In Stanley Lombardo's flinty rendition:

> Hebe slid the bronze, eight-spoked wheels
> Onto the car's iron axle, wheels with pure gold rims
> Fitted with bronze tires, a stunning sight,
> And the hubs spinning on both sides were silver.

Strangely, there is no good film version of Homer's epic. Or perhaps that's not so strange. As cinematic as its techniques may be, *The Iliad* does not lend itself easily to conventional commercial moviemaking. Maybe it would take something like Jacques Rivette's *Out 1*—a thirteen-hour film in which theater groups rehearse avant-garde adaptations of Aeschylus—to capture its sweep and roil. (This is one reason Godard's *Le Mépris* remains the best Homeric movie— among other things, it's a consideration of how one might bring Homer to the screen; Fritz Lang plays himself, hired to adapt *The Odyssey*.) Directors tend to play up the romance angle and tack the sack of Troy from *The Aeneid* onto the end, as in Robert Wise's *Helen of Troy* (1956) and Wolfgang Petersen's *Troy* (2004). As Paul notes, *The Iliad* "does not claim to be 'about' the Trojan War, and it does not matter that it ends before the war does."[64]

Troy is a bad movie, peppered with basic errors and laughable dialogue. But it contains one scene that seems to me to possess genuine Homeric insight. It's the battle between Achilles, played pretty well by Brad Pitt, and Eric Bana's Hector. Achilles is insane with rage and grief over Patroclus—you know the story—and controls the fight from the outset. But at one point, Hector scores a blow, nicking Achilles's breastplate. Achilles looks down at the mark in astonishment. It's just a scratch on the leather, not worth a second thought, but Achilles can't believe it, and you realize—no one has ever penetrated his defenses that far before. No sword point has ever been that close to his flesh. It's a brilliant moment: it tells you how good Hector is, and, even more, how good Achilles is. And in a flash, from a simple glance, you have a sense of these two warriors as titans—the son of a god contending with the son of a king.

This is the sort of effect the late Christopher Logue achieves again and again in *War Music: An Account of Homer's* Iliad, the greatest film adaptation of Homer ever set down on paper. The new edition gathers the poem, written over forty years and published in installments over twenty-five—*War Music* (1981, covering books

16–19); *Kings* (1991, books 1 and 2); *The Husbands* (1995, books 3 and 4); *All Day Permanent Red* (2003, books 5 and 6); *Cold Calls* (2005, books 7–9)—and adds as an appendix *Big Men Falling a Long Way*, editor Christopher Reid's reconstruction of Logue's projected final installment, which contains fragments from books 10 to 24.

It's very far from a translation, by design—Logue, who couldn't read ancient Greek and worked from existing translations, rearranges Homer's material as he pleases and drags the diction into the present by way of Pound's *Cantos*, even borrowing lines from August Kleinzahler. The redoubtable classics scholar Bernard Knox was shocked at the liberties taken in *The Husbands*. It might have helped to think of it as a movie. Indeed, Logue opens with an establishing shot worthy of John Ford:

> Picture the east Aegean sea by night,
> And on a beach aslant its shimmering
> Upwards of 50,000 men
> Asleep like spoons beside their lethal Fleet.

The filmic qualities become explicit at times, infiltrating the poem's vocabulary. The shift of speakers in Achilles's insolent exchange with Agamemnon is produced by "Silence. // Reverse the shot. // Go close. // Hear Agamemnon . . ." After Hector kills Patroclus, as the Greeks mass on the beach to attack: "Close-up on Bombax; 45; fighting since 2." "Quick cuts like these may give / Some definition to the mind's wild eye."

Critics have focused on these cinematic aspects of the poem, but Paul brings out how properly Homeric they are—how *The Iliad* is "primed and *ready* to be made cinematic."[65] Logue's poem, I'd argue, zooms in closer to Homer than the plodding literalism of a version like Richmond Lattimore's, made to "please professors," as Guy Davenport said.[66] Of course lines like these take us far from the Greek text:

> "There's Bubblegum!" "He's out to make his name!"
> "He's charging us!" "He's prancing!" "Get that leap!"
>   THOCK! THOCK!
> "He's in the air!" "Bubblegum's in the air!" "Above the dust!"
>   "He's lying on the sunshine in the air!" "Seeing the
>   Wall!" "The arrows keep him up!"
>   THOCK! THOCK!

And you'll find Kansas in these pages, and Uzis, binoculars, Stalingrad, and Cape Kennedy, "headroom" and guitars, helicopters, airplanes, fly-fishing, gigantic font, and the earth revolving around the sun. But like Brad Pitt's stunned face, *War Music* finds a visual and emotional equivalent for Homer's human realities, as when Achilles looks over the armor Thetis has brought him:

> Spun the holy tungsten like a star between his knees,
> Slitting his eyes against the flare, some said,
> But others thought the hatred shuttered by his lids
> Made him protect the metal.
>
>   His eyes like furnace doors ajar.
>
>   When he had got its weight
> And let its industry assuage his grief:
>   "I'll fight,"
> He said. Simple as that. "I'll fight."
>
>   And so Troy fell.

It doesn't always work. But Logue's reconciliations of idea and image are often perfect.

> Think of a raked sky-wide Venetian blind.
> Add the receding traction of its slats

Of its slats of its slats as a hand draws it up.
Hear the Greek army getting to its feet.

These lines even have a soundtrack, the repeated staccato alliteration of the slats recalling Ginsberg's "boxcars boxcars boxcars."

There are fine passages in the unfinished material culled from Logue's notes—with a title as delicious as *Big Men Falling a Long Way* there would almost have to be—including an initial stab at Brad Pitt vs. Eric Bana, the scene I most lament Logue's not having lived to complete. But welcome as it is, this material is mostly undeveloped and diffuse, and can't add much to our experience of the poem. We can all regret that the poet was unable to undertake his planned rewriting of Homer's famous 130-line description of Achilles's shield, which Logue proposed in his notes to *extend*.

But *War Music* is complete in its way, one of the mad socko follies of the twentieth century, writhing with coarse, fevered life. Logue conveys the terrible rush of war with the guerilla pathos of Samuel Fuller's epigraph to *The Big Red One*: " 'Why are you crying?'—An insane child to a burning tank." Odysseus to Achilles:

> They do not own the swords with which they fight,
> Nor the ships that brought them here.
> Orders are handed down to them in words
> They barely understand.
> They do not give a whit who owns queen Helen.
> Ithaca's mine; Pythia yours; but what are they defending?
> They love you? Yes. They do. They also loved Patroclus.
> And he is dead, they say. Bury the dead, they say.
> A hundred of us singing angels died for every knock
> Patroclus took—so why the fuss?—that's war, they say,
> Who came to eat in Troy and not to prove how much
> Dear friends are missed.
> Yes, they are fools.
> But they are right. Fools often are.

Bury the dead, my lord,
And I will help you pitch Troy in the sea."

Western literature is born in rage. But it is also born in song. μῆνιν and ἀείδω. "Our machine was devastating," Michael Herr wrote of America's profane destruction of Indochina. "And versatile. It could do everything but stop."[67] Logue's Homer makes the machine sing.

HOOKED UP

When I was a wee bairn in the late '70s, a mass-market paperback called *The Poetry of Rock* was often to be found among the macramé and marijuana seeds. This anthology was a weird little bible to me, its concordances the records that were always lying around with their mystically resonant titles—*Aja*, *The Slider*, *Sticky Fingers*, *Dixie Chicken*—and glorious gatefolds. I'd pore over lyric sheets the way Harold Bloom claims he immersed himself as a child in Blake and Hart Crane. I first embarked on literary exegesis at seven or eight, trying to understand what it could mean to know "how many holes it takes to fill the Albert Hall."

Reading *The Poetry of Rock* again decades later, I'm impressed by how self-aware it is. I'd assumed I would find it a kitschy cash-in, radio wisdom for the Castaneda set, full of wimpy crap like "The Sound of Silence." That excretion is indeed to be found within the anthology's pages, but for the most part, editor Richard Goldstein of the *Village Voice* was too savvy to fall for the callow philosophizing of folkies like Paul Simon and Phil Ochs. Goldstein says of the latter's unreadable "Crucifixion" that it is "infuriating in its insistence on expressing everything in allegorical terms." Meanwhile, interpreting Dylan is like "running a U.S.O. in Hanoi"; Procol Harum's lyrics "reek of random allusions and post-graduate funk"; "you can almost feel the lurch of brakes between the lines" of the Beatles' "In My Life."

For Goldstein, rock "poetry" is about the ability "to express the forbidden within the context of the permissible." "Poetry" poetry, on the other hand, can sometimes express the forbidden within the context of the forbidden, because it doesn't aspire to go platinum. (The same could be said of punk, I suppose.) Context is, of course, why the answer to the tedious question "Are lyrics poetry?" has to be "It depends." Goldstein notes that "mere linearity can destroy a rock lyric," and claims, despite his anthology's title, that it's a mistake to expect pop lyrics "to move like a poem."

The point is pop music is *music*, duh, and without the Klaxon and clamor of guitars and beats, the words don't really rock and roll.

Heard in certain ways, song lyrics are obviously a form of poetry; in other respects, it seems worthwhile to preserve a distinction. I have collections of the lyrics of W. S. Gilbert, Stephen Foster, Cole Porter, and Stephen Sondheim. What would be the point of denying these lyricists the honorific of "poet"? And I can think of songs by Randy Newman (early), Leonard Cohen (late), Laurie Anderson, and Biggie Smalls that I'd have no problem calling poems.

Still, I've been stranded in the dead waters of Joni Mitchell's "Woodstock" or some other well-mannered token in a literature anthology (Morrissey's execrable "Cemetry Gates" and Mos Def's "Hip Hop" in the most recent *Norton Introduction to Literature*) often enough to question the motivation to enshrine these songs. There's something feebly earnest about anthologies like *The Poetry of Rock* or Adam Bradley and Andrew DuBois's recent *Anthology of Rap*. Does Clipse really need to be rescued from the ghetto of popular culture? I'd say anyone who can write like this—"All the snow on the timepiece confusin' 'em/All the snow on the concrete Peruvian"—is doing fine without Norton's imprimatur.

Anyway, at least half the force of these lines is in Pusha's delivery: he shakes each syllable in his teeth to break its spine against the click-clack machine rhythms of the backing track. A great tune, a killer solo, and a perfect beat can render terrible lyrics irrelevant, as Neil Young's career proves.

Lyrics work best when they aren't straining to achieve poetic effect (ask Jackson Browne). Springsteen became a great song-writer when he stopped aping Dylan and found the poetry in a "sixty-nine Chevy with a 396 / Fuelie heads and a Hurst on the floor." Tori Amos's best lyric is about wanting to smack Oliver Stone.

At the moment the lyricist who impresses me most is Jason Is-bell, formerly of the Drive-By Truckers. Although he wrote some of that Skynyrd-proud band's best numbers, his first few solo records came on too safe. But the songs on his fourth album, *Southeastern*, make the music around them on the radio sound like jingles for Discount Carpet Warehouse. Partly that's because his voice is so idiosyncratically gorgeous that he could sing the surgeon general's warning on a pack of smokes and make you cry.

But it's also because of lines like these, from "Different Days": "You can strip in Portland from the day you turn sixteen / You got one thing to sell and benzodiazepine." Isbell knows how his lyrics work in ways that have nothing to do with their meaning. "I step into a shop to buy a postcard for a girl" sounds full of emotion on "Relatively Easy," but why? For one thing, it's perfectly iambic, with a sonic pileup of *ss* and *ps*.

Like the Clipse lyrics above, Isbell's operate at the phonemic level, sounds picking up and pinging off one another: at "Christmastime" someone's "woman took the kids and he took Klonopin / Enough to kill a man of twice his size." Listen to the way "woman" resonates with "Klonopin," "Chris" with "kids" and "kill," "time" with "twice" and "size."

This is what Roger Miller called "hooked up," as Dave Hickey relates in his entry on "The Song in Country Music" in Greil Marcus and Werner Sollors's *A New Literary History of America*. It's the single best discussion of song lyrics I know.

When I asked Roger Miller what it was about [Hank] Williams's songwriting that touched him, he said, "Meticulous. They're meticulous and all hooked up." When I asked him what this meant, he . . . sang half a verse of "Me and Bobby McGee," a song by Kris Kristofferson and Fred Foster that Miller had discovered and recorded first.

> Busted flat in Baton Rouge
> Headed for the trains.
> Feelin' nearly faded as my jeans.

"That's hooked up," Miller said. "I love the 'as' that picks up 'flat' and 'bat.'" And "faded" picks up "headed" and "trains."

Hickey asked Waylon Jennings about Williams's songs, and Jennings "sang lines from two or three of them and showed me how the sounding of the consonants moved from the front to the back of the mouth so the vowels were always singable." The songwriter Harlan Howard explained how "eight short lines" of Williams's "Cold, Cold Heart" are "invisibly held together by fifteen internal *r* phonemes. . . . 'Nobody notices this,' Howard said. 'That's the idea, but once these words are put together this way, they won't come apart.'"

That's important: you don't necessarily attend consciously to these elements in the song; you're not meant to. They're glue, holding the verse in your memory, sticking the words to your ears. And just as poets who write in meter don't need to count off beats on their fingers, because they have internalized the mechanism through long practice, a songwriter can lay these units down without having to plot out the placement of *r* phonemes as he writes. "Once you learned how to do it, you couldn't not do it," Hickey explains.[68]

This is the most significant way in which songs differ from poems—they're intended to be heard, while poems for some time have been written primarily for the eye. As Christopher Ricks puts it in his brilliant and annoying *Dylan's Visions of Sin*, "the eye can always simply see more than it is reading, looking at; the ear cannot, in this sense (given what the sense of hearing is), hear a larger span than it is receiving. This makes the relation of an artist like Dylan to song and ending crucially different from the relation of an artist like Donne or Larkin to ending."[69]

Poems, that is to say, are no less complex than a hooked-up country song (or shouldn't be—God knows they are, often enough). But a poem's hooks are spatial in a way a song's can't be—you see its ending coming—unless the song is reduced to its printed lyrics, in which case it's not a song anymore. Lyrics are just one moving part of the machine we call a song—without music and voice, they just sit there, no matter how meticulously crafted they might be. So whether lyrics are poetry is a question that doesn't require an answer, or has too many to bother with. It's enough that we have songs—"domestic magic," Hickey calls Hank's—and can sing.

VISIBLE REPUBLIC

Gentlemen, he said, I don't need your organization. And surely Bob Dylan, one of the wealthiest and most successful artists in history, did not require the imprimatur of the Nobel Committee for Literature at the Swedish Academy. Nevertheless, here we were, on the morning of October 13, 2016, arguing about whether it made a lick of sense for a popular songwriter—even *the* popular songwriter—to be awarded this most prestigious of literary prizes. Was there precedent? There was not: Every single previous winner of the Nobel Prize in Literature—even Winston Churchill (1953)—won for writings that were primarily, um, writings.

Twitter was aquiver with approbation and disdain. Stephen King and Salman Rushdie were pro, Hari Kunzru and Gary Shteyngart were anti. I was briefly made livid by something the critic Jody Rosen tweeted: "Cute, but songwriting isn't literature." This is not true. "Sir Patrick Spens" is literature. And if the blues is "primarily a verse form and secondarily a way of making music," as Amiri Baraka wrote in *Blues People*, surely the same could be said of rap.[70]

But I soon realized Rosen's claim was a hyperbolic version of a point I actually agree with, which he clarified in subsequent tweets. Rosen was opposing the notion that popular music needs to be validated by literary honorifics, while I was rejecting the notion that popular music *can't* be literary. These positions aren't mutually exclusive.

And decades after the much-hyped, much-distorted advent of barbarian postmodernism at the gates of the academy, Rosen's argument is probably the more relevant one. That popular art—film and comics and hip-hop—is no less worthy of sustained intellectual engagement than literature (which is at any rate an amorphous and contested category) is fairly well established by now, despite the fulminations of Harold Bloom. It's not that pop music doesn't deserve a Nobel Prize but that pop music doesn't need it. (And, uh, guys? John Ashbery is still alive.)

Furthermore, if the thing had to be given to a North American musician—and my feeds were filled with folks proposing boring alternatives like Joni Mitchell and Leonard Cohen—why not one of the black pioneers without whom Robert Zimmerman would just be an annoying amalgam of Woody Guthrie and Jack Kerouac? Chuck Berry, as Rosen suggested, or Little Richard? Or why not Sly Stone? Or if we're really talking "great poets," as the Swedish Academy's permanent secretary had it, Rakim or Chuck D or Ghostface Killah?

Well, because demographics, to put it politely. Boomer hagiography of Dylan should be its own Nobel category. Have you heard that Dylan went electric over fifty years ago, and some mope shouted "Judas"? If not, allow me to recommend a few dozen books on the subject. The academics, especially, are full of passionate intensity. Christopher Ricks has written some of the smartest poetry analysis you'll ever read, and *Dylan's Visions of Sin* is very smart. It also sounds like this:

> And Dylan is energy incarnate. Energy is Activity. . . . The opposite of slothful? "Diligent" is the opposing term that is everywhere in the Book of Proverbs (which Dylan knows like the back of God's hand). O O O O that Dylanesque rag. It's so elegant. So intelligent. So Dyligent. Never negligent.[71]

The day after the announcement, the *Times* ran an article I refuse to read with the headline "Bob Dylan 101: A Harvard Professor

Has the Coolest Class on Campus." Dylan has exacerbated this tendency by writing (in addition to some of the best lyrics in the popular tradition) a lot of self-consciously literary gunk ("Ezra Pound and T. S. Eliot / Fighting in the captain's tower"—Dad, please, you're embarrassing me).

But our age is characterized by, in Bifo Berardi's words, "an excess of speed of the infosphere in relation to the ability of elaboration of the brain," so instant reactions are demanded, with little or no time for thoughtful reflection.[72] In other words, just when I was starting to feel that popular song hardly needed to be defended, the think pieces began to appear. Most were simply banal (the *New Yorker* invited a bunch of writers to pick their favorite Dylan lyrics). But Stephen Metcalf, writing for *Slate*, went all in, proclaiming that "Bob Dylan is a musician, not a poet."[73] To prove it, he quoted the poet Richard Wilbur:

> The heavens jumped away,
> Bursting the cincture of the zodiac,
> Shot flares with nothing left to say
> To us, not coming back

Followed by lines from Dylan's "Up to Me" beginning "Oh, the Union Central is pullin' out and the orchids are in bloom." According to Metcalf, Dylan's lines "are colloquial, spare, painterly, and without the accompanying music, inert." Wilbur's poem "is poetry," Dylan's song is just "lyrics."

"Colloquial, spare, painterly" could describe some of the best poems in the language, including several by Frank O'Hara, James Schuyler, Elizabeth Bishop, Gwendolyn Brooks, Lorine Niedecker, Allen Ginsberg, Tom Pickard—I could go on and on. If Dylan's lines aren't poetry, neither is this, from a poem by Langston Hughes:

> My old time daddy
> Came back home last night.

His face was pale and
His eyes didn't look just right.

He says, "Mary, I'm
Comin' home to you—
So sick and lonesome
I don't know what to do."

What Metcalf is really saying, whether he means to or not, is that poetry is about fancy stuff like the cincture of the zodiac, not the Union Central pullin' out.

It's no accident that both Dylan and Hughes draw on the blues, which draws on Christian rhetoric, which represented for Erich Auerbach the merging of the high and low styles of classical antiquity. I don't think Metcalf means to denigrate lyrics as such—there's nothing wrong with just writing lyrics—and I don't mean to, either. But the hierarchy he establishes is invidious in itself. Yes, Dylan is a poet—*and* a musician *and* a lyricist. "Poet" is just an honorific we grant for different reasons at different times (take a look at how elastic Shelley gets with it in "A Defence of Poetry").

And yet—so what? Dylan's honorific-withholding detractors do have a point, one Ellen Willis made best in the pages of *Cheetah* in 1967: "Words or rhymes that seem gratuitous in print often make good musical sense, and Dylan's voice, an extraordinary interpreter of emotion . . . makes vague lines clear. . . . The result is a unity of sound and word."[74] It's the music, the *performance*. (Willis also wrote that "Dylan's music is not inspired," which would be nonsense even if she hadn't been writing just after the hat trick of *Bringing It All Back Home*, *Highway 61 Revisited*, and *Blonde on Blonde*.)

As Albert Murray wrote of blues audiences in *Stomping the Blues*, as if contradicting Baraka, "most of their goose pimples and all of their finger snapping and foot tapping are produced by the sound far more often than by the meaning of the words."[75] This is what Rosen and Metcalf were getting at, and the argument doesn't require denying that songwriting can be literature or that songwriters can be poets. The poet Joshua Clover put it like this (also on Twitter): "1. of course songs can be lit 2. Dylan is an astonishing artist 3. it's not the lit part that makes him astonishing."

This truth crept into what was by far the best response piece, Greil Marcus's appreciation in the *New York Times*. Marcus began by sweeping the problem aside: "But whether Mr. Dylan is a poet—yes, he is being compared right now to Sappho, Homer, the great bards who *sang*—has never been an interesting question." He's right. But that is the question the Swedish Academy raised by giving a literary prize to someone whose words would never have meant so much to so many if they hadn't been set to such inspired music.

Marcus gets at what is most mind-buckling about the songwriter when he considers a performance of "Highway 61 Revisited" by Dylan and the Band on their 1974 tour (during which they recorded the live album *Before the Flood*, a colossal document that still renders all criticism two-dimensional):

> The song may have reached its most intense pitch in a performance with the Band in Oakland, Calif., in 1974, when a broken riff from the guitarist Robbie Robertson between verses shot Mr. Dylan's attack for the final stanza—about staging the next world war between bleachers set up on Highway 61, the road that now runs from Minnesota to New Orleans—into a realm of vehemence, of *Watch out!* that the song had never known before.[76]

That's it, that's the thing—Dylan isn't words. He's words plus Robertson's uncanny *awk*, drummer Levon Helm's cephalopodic clatter, the thin, wild mercury of his voice. Listen to him sing "Blind Willie McTell," from *The Bootleg Series, Volumes 1–3*—voice swinging and creaking like magnolia trees in a storm—and tell me that what matters about this man is *literature*.

Nevertheless, Dylan joins the company of Pearl Buck and William Golding, while Ashbery remains in that of Tolstoy, Henry James, Proust, Joyce, Gertrude Stein, Wallace Stevens, Virginia Woolf, Langston Hughes, Borges, Nabokov, James Baldwin, and Chinua Achebe. The single best response to the *zomg dylan won the nobel* hullabaloo came from the poet Alice Notley, who simply retweeted some Dickinsonian lines she'd posted in 2014:

> I gave myself the Nobel Prize for Literature—
> Without the check—and also the
> Medal of Freedom. I deserved both
> of them; & now I have them.

"

ARE YOU SMEARED WITH THE
JUICE OF CHERRIES?

The first line of Robert Hass's first collection, *Field Guide*, which won the Yale Series of Younger Poets Award in 1972, is "I won't say much for the sea." This offhand repurposing of idiom, funny and insightful, is characteristic of his poems—of course he goes on to say a million things for and about the sea. *Field Guide* was acclaimed, as each succeeding book would be, for Hass's facility in translating into poems what is ridiculously referred to as "the natural world." In the first three poems alone, we find: steelhead, mushrooms, apricots, gulls, sea cucumbers, slugs, a walnut tree, ironwood, waxwings, pyracantha, cliffs, bluffs, artichokes, a salt creek, owl's clover, lupine, berries, hawthorns, laurels, "clams, abalones, cockles, chitons, crabs," salmon, swamp grass, and a skunk. The preoccupation with nonhuman life is inextricable from a compulsive onomatomania: "Earth-wet, slithery, / we drifted toward the names of things"; "I recite the hard / explosive names of birds: / egret, killdeer, bittern, tern." This impulse is explained, sort of, in "Maps":

> Of all the laws
> that bind us to the past
> the names of things are
> stubbornest

When Hass's pintails and blue-winged teals are lined up in a row, the deftness of his observations almost rivals that of the haiku masters he has so memorably translated: in a restaurant's tank, "coppery lobsters scuttling over lobsters." But as the above verse suggests, Hass is also given to pedantic soothsaying, telling the reader *how it is* in tones that suggest he is just slightly winded from having jogged down the slopes of Parnassus. The poetry takes on the tenor of the lecture hall, the quality of prose statement: *Of all the laws that bind us to the past, the names of things are stubbornest*. Is this true? Is it even meaningful?

This register contributes to the dewy piety that makes it impossible to read many Hass poems with a straight face. The metaphor "jump the shark" has itself long since jumped the shark, but in its spirit I'd like to propose a new phrase to describe the moment when a poem goes hilariously off the rails. This phrase is "hating the cunt," and I take it from *Field Guide*'s "In Weather," in which a man's "heavy cock wields, / rises, spits seed / at random":

> It descends to women occasionally
> with contempt and languid tenderness.
> I tried to hate my wife's cunt,
> the sweet place where I rooted.

When discussing a poem in which the poet is so enamored of himself and his sincerity that he is rendered quite tone-deaf to the comic pseudo-profundity of his lines, one might say something like, "The third stanza really hates the cunt." In the next section of the same poem, Hass is lying in bed listening to the mating cries of owls until he decides to imitate the wail:

> of owls, ecstatic
> in the winter trees, *twoo, twoo*.

I drew long breaths.
My wife stirred in our bed.

So let's see: you're already trying to hate your wife's, er, companion-able hole, and now she has to put up with you making *owl noises* in the middle of the night? Let the woman sleep!

Like Mary Oliver and Billy Collins—in their different ways—Hass has made a career out of flattering middlebrow sensibilities with cheap mystery. Unlike those poets, Hass has real talent. *The Apple Trees at Olema* is a frustrating blend of banality and brilliance. The second volume, *Praise*, now reads as a primer in late-'70s period style, the kind of laid-back beach koans that led people to believe Galway Kinnell's "The Bear" was a good poem. There are more ber-ries, more naming of flowers, more embarrassingly tin-eared war-bling in the demotic:

> It is different in kind from a man and the pale woman
> he fucks in the ass underneath the stars
> because it is summer and they are full of longing
> and sick of birth.

Does ass fucking really require such a high-minded justification? Upon being told someone is fucking someone else in the ass, has anyone ever responded, "What! Why?" I regret to inform the reader that Hass goes on to compare this sex act to the sacking of Troy.

Hass's most famous poem, "Meditation at Lagunitas," also suc-cumbs to his fatal need to elevate everything to the phosphorescent plane of longing. It begins vividly by tweaking a worn catchphrase into literality:

> All the new thinking is about loss.
> In this it resembles all the old thinking.

> The idea, for example, that each particular erases
> the luminous clarity of a general idea. That the clown-
> faced woodpecker probing the dead sculpted trunk
> of that black birch is, by his presence,
> some tragic falling off from a first world
> of undivided light.

Here, the poet is arguing *against* the deadening tendency to force ordinary particulars into luminosity. A woodpecker is allowed to be a woodpecker, and those who would derive allegory from its presence are seduced by intellectual fashion. Within a few lines, Hass is remembering "a woman / I made love to": "I felt a violent wonder at her presence / like a thirst for salt, for my childhood river / with its island willows." He's savvy; he knows that "it hardly had to do with her." But by the end of the poem, which everyone knows—"Such tenderness, those afternoons and evenings, / saying *blackberry, blackberry, blackberry*"—you begin to realize that Hass's particulars are often subsumed into the general because he thinks that merely intoning the names of things can replace the hard work of description. A brief poem in *Field Guide* ends:

> On the oak table
>   filets of sole
> stewing in the juice of tangerines,
>   slices of green pepper
>   on a bone-white dish.

This is a list of stuff in Hass's kitchen. If Jack Spicer's perfect poem had an infinitely small vocabulary, Hass's contains only the words "ripe blackberries." (This is, in fact, the entirety of the twelfth section of "The Beginning of September.")

But although the preciousness remains an irritant ("the floribunda are / heavy with the richness and sadness of Europe"—oh really?), in the three books that follow *Praise* Hass is often charmingly aware of, and thus able to subvert, his own windy inclinations. The title poem of *Human Wishes* (1989) begins:

> This morning the sun rose over the garden wall and a rare
> blue sky leaped from east to west. Man is altogether desire,
> say the Upanishads. Worth anything, a blue sky, says Mr.
> Acker, the Shelford gardener. Not altogether. In the end.
> Last night on television the ethnologist and the cameraman
> watched with hushed wonder while the chimpanzee carefully
> stripped a willow branch and inserted it into the anthill. He
> desired red ants.

The first sentence is not promising, but what follows is terrific, in part because the gardener's platitude deftly exposes the hollowness of the opening. The poet's aside—"Not altogether"—responds to the Upanishads but also to Mr. Acker's bland assertion, and that puffery about "a rare blue sky" is deflated by association. Hass has jumped a few levels of the game. The bit about the nature program is just as astute: not "there was an ethnologist" or "we saw a show where an ethnologist." The definite articles produce an immediacy that is reinforced by the lack of framing. There is always an ethnologist on television somewhere, watching a chimp.

Human Wishes' prose poems inaugurated a genial talkiness that also enlivens the best work in *Sun Under Wood* (1996) and *Time and Materials* (2007). The poems in these later collections are often anecdotal, playful even when politically outraged, skillfully polished in order to appear offhand, attentive to their own processes. Hass has an engaging way of seeming to switch tracks, often by tossing in a seemingly random historical factoid, as in these lines from "Churchyard":

When deer in the British Isles were forced to live in the open because of heavy foresting, it stunted them. The red deer who lived in the Scottish highlands a thousand years ago were a third larger than the present animal.

Hass is at his best when, as here, he is at his most casual. "The Miwoks called it Moon of the Only Credit Card" is not a line that would have occurred to the young man who wrote *Field Guide*. He cultivates a sense of having jotted down something that flitted through his thoughts, without ever straining after the unconvincing illusion of stream of consciousness. A poem in *Time and Materials* ends by musing of Whitman, "He was in love with a trolley conductor / In the summer of—what was it?—1867? 1868?" Another poem, "I Am Your Waiter Tonight and My Name Is Dmitri," begins:

> Is, more or less, the title of a poem by John Ashbery and has
> No investment in the fact that you can get an adolescent
> Of the human species to do almost anything

This is "why they are tromping down a road in Fallujah / In combat gear and a hundred and fifteen degrees of heat." These lines are both funny and furious (also unfair to Ashbery's delightful "My Name Is Dimitri," which, by the way, is spelled by Ashbery with three *i*s), but did we really need the Horatian tagline that follows? (Take a guess.) At times this didacticism becomes preachy, and Hass sounds like Bono lecturing the UN:

> In the first twenty years
> of the twentieth century 90 percent of war deaths were the
> deaths of combatants. In the last twenty years of the twentieth century 90 percent of war deaths were deaths of civilians.

There are imaginable responses to these facts. The nations of the world could stop setting an example for suicide bombers. They could abolish the use of land mines.

We appreciate your input, Professor Hass. We will take it under advisement.

FREDERICK SEIDEL'S BAD TASTE

A popular clip on YouTube shows a local news reporter trying to interview a costume-shop owner who'd been charged with cyberstalking. The woman is dressed as a giant rabbit and refuses to take the reporter seriously. When he asks her to remove "the bunny head" she complies, only to reveal that she is wearing a vampire mask underneath. My interview with Frederick Seidel, ostensibly for the *Village Voice*, was marginally less successful than this.

In keeping with his perverse ways, Seidel agreed to answer only two questions. One of my questions ponderously involved the received sense, here in the States, that poetry is no longer a vital cultural force, a feeling further emphasized by the National Endowment for the Art's (NEA) recent announcement that in 2008 almost ninety-two percent of American adults had read no poetry at all. What role, I wondered, can poetry play in such an environment? I had in mind something like Allen Grossman's admission that he is uncertain what poetry "can *now mean* in the context of the actual human task."77 But Seidel simply responded with Samuel Johnson's line, borrowed from Sidney (who got it from Horace), that poetry must please and instruct. Fair enough. So what are his poems instructing us in or to do? "That's for you to say." At least I think this is how the conversation went: when I sat down to transcribe the interview, I discovered, not without a sense of relief, that I had inserted the microphone cord into the wrong jack on the tape recorder. Only my questions had been preserved.

A friend suggested I should just have asked: "Why are you a monster?" For it is wonderfully apt that this particular interview should have crashed so spectacularly: Seidel is, as everyone notices, a terrifying poet, who writes terrifying poems.

"Everything in the poems is true," Seidel told *New York* magazine in 2006. "You should take them at face value." Richard Poirier provides the de rigueur response: "Fred's created a character named Frederick Seidel that has little to do with who he is."[78] In a review of Seidel's *Cosmos Poems* and *Life on Earth*, Calvin Bedient likewise assures us that Seidel's "poetic 'I' " is "fictive and hyperbolic."[79] Something about Seidel's poetry moves critics to foreground the familiar claim that the speaker of a poem is not identical with the poet. For what could it mean to take lines like these, from "Letter to the Editors of *Vogue*," at "face value"?

> I am drinking gasoline
> To stay awake
> In the midst of so much
> Murder.
>
> My daughter squeaks and squeaks
> Like a mouse screaming in a trap,
> Dangling from the cat who makes her come
> When he does it to her.

What would it mean to inhabit Seidel's assertion rather than reflexively dismiss it, to suspend our learned doubt about the "speakers" of poems? It can't mean accepting everything in the poems as literally true: I doubt even Seidel drinks gasoline. Taking the poems at face value does not require us to take them as factual autobiographical reports. Rather, I contend that Seidel gives himself over to grotesquerie, caricature, and hyperbole, a strategy of outsized scale, in order both to offer a critique of morality based on taste and to claim for himself an extreme form of agency.

Specifically, Seidel conducts an amplification of affect beyond what we might legitimately ascribe to ordinary persons. Every critic of Seidel has located him within the Lowellian tradition of masculinist confession. But if the literary historical assumption about confession is that it institutes a norm of subjectivity, Seidel's work helps us to see that this norm's contours have always been extreme rather than normative. Or, to put it another way, Seidel's hyperbole, like Freud's and Nietzsche's, encodes an intuition that the extreme *is* the norm rather than a deviation from it. This is a corollary of the premise from which Seidel begins: that we live in a culture of almost unlimited suffering, a culture whose capacity to produce guilt and shame is infinite. To respond adequately to the infernal conditions of modernity requires what George Puttenham, in 1589, termed "*Hiperbole*, or the Ouer reacher, otherwise called the loud lyer," the "immoderate excesse" of poetic speech.[80] As Seidel has it, "Civilized life is actually about too much." His lurid hyperbole is a way of negotiating the problem of personhood in an impersonally violent world.

Seidel's confessions sometimes take a plausibly Lowellian form: "A naked woman my age is a total nightmare," he writes. This is readable *as* (although not only as) confession—as if pronounced, that is, with chagrin, in acknowledgment that one is in error. But such moments, although outrageous, compete for space with more telling ones. Seidel imagines a terrorist blowing up the Chunnel train, along with "a flock of Japanese schoolgirls ready to be fucked / In their school uniforms in paradise." He is given to schoolboy blurts like "Shit with a cunt! / The prince was blunt. / Shit with a cunt. // Cunt with a dick!" Here we find Seidel reveling in unacceptable social attitudes—whatever schoolgirls might actually do, a fairly uncontroversial morality disallows describing them as "ready to be fucked," especially when they are about to be murdered (in a vignette of stereotyped Islamist fanaticism)—and a kind of infantile scatology, Tourette's syndrome as nonsense verse. These ejaculations are characteristic of Seidel's work, and they undermine the moral scaffolding on which an earnest Lowellian confession (which, however theatrical, solicits expiation) would seem to depend. However indebted to Robert Lowell he might be in other ways, it would be a category mistake to see Seidel as truly "confessional," precisely because he "confesses" in order to offend against the norms of taste, to revel in, rather than repent of, the sins he has committed. He's more like the movie villain who brags of his crimes in order to make the hero squirm.

Indeed, the rehearsal of historical pain in his own person for which Lowell is chastised by Marjorie Perloff and other critics is a form of theater that Seidel will stand on its head. He rehearses his personal crudities in the viscera of history. Given just how crude and visceral his poetry can be, such that some critics are tempted to conclude it is all a put-on, it's worth thinking about the term *face value*. The *OED* defines it as "the value printed or depicted on a coin, banknote, ticket, etc., especially when less than the actual value; (*fig.*) the apparent character, nature, worth, or meaning of a person or thing." On this definition, Seidel is directing us not to look for some "actual" meaning behind the poems' "apparent" meaning: their appearance is their reality. But this means we should be especially careful about what we take to be their apparent meaning. We should pay particular attention to the language of the poems, even when that means looking at what disgusts us, as Seidel's speaker does in some lines that do seem to seek absolution: "I hate seeing the anus of a beautiful woman. / I should not be looking. It should not be there."

Poirier would have us believe that the "actual value" of these lines, as opposed to their "apparent character," depends on the recognition that (what might seem) their callow investment in surfaces "has little to do with who" Seidel is. But the indictment of surfaces is self-directed: "*I should not be looking*" at the woman's anus. And even as the petulance of "It should not be there" expresses a wholly impotent protest against the entropic processes of nature—a futile desire that beauty not be marred by reminders of its origins in and eventual return to decay and waste—it more complexly confirms that self-indictment: it should not be there in my field of vision, I should (but do not) have the decency to avert my gaze. The face value of the anus is staring him in the face—he stares into it and sees himself as if it were a mirror: *I'm the asshole*.

The value, then, of his outrageousness is to be had by taking it seriously. When Lowell admits that "Everybody's tired of my turmoil," it's possible to read him as truly self-deprecating. Seidel, on the other hand, despite gestures toward self-deprecation, rarely lets us forget not only that he really is an asshole, but also that he is not about to apologize for it. To ask whether this is a persona is beside the point, or it is to overestimate the distancing effect of personae. Isobel Armstrong has astutely problematized the status of Browning's personae in *Men and Women* by suggesting that the poet is "extraordinarily faithful" to a Benthamite conception of aesthetic fictionality. On this view, a fiction must be dealt with "as if it were real simply because it has entered substantively into experience by existing at all." By not writing in propria persona, Browning builds the politico-ideological problem of agency "into the very structure of the poem *as* a problem."[81] Rather than absolving the poet of personal commitment to his words, persona dramatizes the problems of selfhood, the questions of where and how agency inheres. The sheer force of the personality on display renders toothless the resort to persona as a way of excusing the poet's seeming depravity. Seidel's poetry, in the words of Armstrong's reading, "declares itself insistently, almost raucously, with a kind of ravenous energy which asks to be confronted."[82] What that energy asks to be confronted *with* is the reader's taste—his or her disgust and offense—to suggest that that taste provides the unexamined foundation of a morality that serves as a facade disguising hard truths.

To understand this mechanism of Seidel's poetry, as vehicle of both moral critique and self-empowerment, consider Alexander Nehamas's analysis of Nietzsche's use of hyperbole, which is often insulting and in bad taste, but which never lets his readers forget that the argument they are getting involved in is always in more than one sense personal. . . . It is true that Nietzsche's texts, compared to many other philosophical works, often say too much; but this comparison leaves open the possibility that the excess may after all be even more accurate than the literal standard, which may itself come to be seen as a trope in its own right, as a litotes or understatement.

Nehamas goes on to contrast Nietzsche's "self-aggrandizing, aristocratic, esoteric manner" with Socrates's self-effacement, suggesting that the German's style has the effect of heightening the sense that the reader is in the presence of a *personality*.[83] Nietzsche's hyperbole is affective *and* rhetorical, but it's important to note that his hyperbole is an entailment of his philosophy, not an exaggeration or evasion of its conclusions. His philosophy requires excessive affect because it holds that the excessive is not a limit case but the only adequate response to a world that is "a monster of force."[84] In such a world, dialectics is "a symptom of decadence," decorum the recourse of cowards.[85] Seidel's hyperbole has the effect of Nietzsche's "magnificent exuberance of a young beast of prey that plays gracefully and, as it plays, dismembers."[86] In Seidel's poetry, to exuberantly inhabit the world is to participate in moral atrocity and dismemberment—"Horror, horror, I hear it, head chopped off"— and the critique Seidel proffers lambasts us for turning away. Like Nietzsche, Seidel reevaluates a dominant ideology of morality from the perspective of one who sees clearly into the abyss of modernity.

The point is that something authentic or essential seems to be unearthed about both the world and the self in extremity. Seidel's hyperbole and excess are amplifications of the literal. More precisely, they are a way of saying, with Theodor Adorno, "The barbaric *is* the literal."[87] For Seidel, then, hyperbole is a means of confronting the world on its own terms, of constructing an affective vocabulary adequate to the world's barbarism. It is also therefore a means of producing personality in a specific relationship to shame. Seidel seeks to move entirely beyond shame, to be literally shameless, making the most barbaric aspects of the self the sources of its power, presence, and even delight. According to Eve Kosofsky Sedgwick, drawing here on developmental psychology, shame is "the affect that most defines the space wherein a sense of self will develop."[88] With this in mind, I want to consider some of Seidel's most offensive lines in order to read his commitment to inflating and dramatizing his own worst impulses—to a performance of his own shamelessness—as a way of confronting a moral dependence on taste and sensibility.

Specifically, Seidel's "bad taste" poses a challenge to his readers (as well as to himself) to defend their unthinking willingness to be guided by their tastes. He insists on the triviality of questions of artistic propriety in order to demonstrate the inadequacy of the affects surrounding taste—particularly when it takes the form of horror or disgust—as a response to a world that presents itself, to Seidel as to others, as "a killing field." "I stick my heart on a stick / To toast it over the fire," Seidel writes in "Mr. Delicious." His heart "blackens to / Campfire goo" while "choo-choo- / Train puffs of white smoke rise" and "trains waddle full of cattle to the camps." "Ovens cremate fields of human cow" and "fields of human snow."

"Mr. Delicious" both crassly refuses and boldly confirms Adorno's shopworn proposition that to write lyric poetry after Auschwitz is barbaric. It is worth imagining, because it is imaginable, a claim that the "actual value" of "Mr. Delicious" is as an exercise in moral edification, mimetic of the atrocity the poem describes: the language one uses with children ("choo-choo train") seems grotesquely out of place, until one reflects that children *were* grotesquely out of place in the death camps. The seemingly innocuous word *campfire*, with its connotations of Scouts munching marshmallows, glints off the gold teeth of corpses reduced to ash. The point of the poem would then be something like: the twentieth century has tainted language itself, cremated it—which was Adorno's point. *Of course* poetic language is incommensurate to the horrors of the Holocaust, Seidel says—and here's how incommensurate it is. I can't even write a poem about it, I can only try to show, hyperbolically, how obscene any attempt to poeticize the event must remain.

But this reading, which would make Seidel into an edgier Steven Spielberg, seems adequate neither to the gleeful energies with which the poem violates propriety nor to the perversely clichéd subject matter. These lines baffle any attempt to read them as conducting redemptive political work. Seidel's hewing to the standard imagery of chimneys should instruct us that he is not really trying to tell us anything about the murder of European Jewry. The Holocaust, precisely because it has become the archetype of the horror and absurdity of political violence, lends itself too easily to representation, at the risk of triteness—which is to say, it *resists* representation, even of the subversive, antinomian variety Seidel attempts here. In fact, to say this much is already a cliché. Seidel recognizes this, flags it, by reaching for his images only as far as the nearest docudrama—cattle cars, the smoke of crematoria. When we examine his 9/11 poems, we encounter a similarly clichéd representation of an atrocity already almost illegible behind its scrim of clichés: the planes approaching the towers, the flames, the collapsing buildings—no detail not immediately accessible to anyone whose imagination and memory extend no further than televised news footage. He is, we might say, shameless in his exploitation of atrocities that have already passed over into the banality of popularization.

Instead of dismissing this as an aesthetic defect, however, I want to ask what sort of aesthetic defect it is—or, rather, what effect is intended by means of aesthetic defect. "I stick my heart on a stick": what will be skewered in this poem is precisely the sentimentality found in what Blake stylizes as "the human heart," and the *taste* of that heart. Seidel sneers at our refinement, our sensibility, our taste—an entire morality that rests on these—toasts it over the fire to demonstrate its gooey insubstantiality. Indeed, the dimension of the

poem most disagreeable to good taste is perhaps not the inappropriately jovial tone but Seidel's very aestheticization of the horror. The
cattle cars "waddle" in an inane pun, as if they and not their human
cargo were likened to cattle, and the human cows become snow, the
white ash of their transubstantiated flesh drifting across the fields.
This is rather effectively *poetic*, a nice elaboration of imagery that
I, for one, find quite pleasing—and which I therefore, in turn, find
quite distasteful. That is, all these images (the heart as toasted marsh-
mallow, the packed, waddling cattle cars en route to concentration
camps) are wholly poetic both in their *form* (what are the boundaries
of impermissible comparison?) and their *content*. The heart has been
toasted and eaten before, after all—in Baudelaire's "Causerie," and
in the first sonnet of *La Vita Nuova*:

> [Love] seemed like one who is full of joy, and had
> My heart within his hand, and on his arm
> My lady, with a mantle round her, slept;
> Whom (having wakened her) anon he made
> To eat that heart; she ate, as fearing harm.
> Then he went out; and as he went, he wept.[89]

Or, perhaps more to the point, Edward Trelawny on Shelley's fu-
neral:

> The fire was so fierce as to produce a white heat on the iron,
> and to reduce its contents to grey ashes. The only portions that
> were not consumed were some fragments of bones, the jaw,
> and the skull, but what surprised us all, was that the heart re-
> mained entire. In snatching this relic from the fiery furnace,
> my hand was severely burnt; and had any one seen me do the
> act I should have been put into quarantine.[90]

It is not, then, that the heart is being cooked and eaten that is
objectionable, even within the context of a poetic representation of

the Holocaust. It is the content of the image, its gooey incongruity with the subject matter, that so affronts taste. It is, in other words, a *goofy* image, wholly inappropriate to the gravity of the occasion—especially considering how many very real human hearts were actually consumed in the ovens. Adorno warns that artistic representations of the Holocaust,

> by turning suffering into images, harsh and uncompromising though they are . . . wounds the shame we feel in the presence of the victims. For these victims are used to create something, works of art, that are thrown to the consumption of a world which destroyed them. The so-called artistic representation of the sheer physical pain of people beaten to the ground by rifle-butts contains, however remotely, the power to elicit enjoyment out of it. . . . The aesthetic principle of stylization . . . make[s] an unthinkable fate appear to have had some meaning; it is transfigured, something of its horror is removed.[91]

He then argues that such representations have nonetheless a dialectical value, for "no art which tried to evade [the victims] could confront the claims of justice." But do I need to say that Seidel appears uninterested in the claims of justice? "Mr. Delicious" is not *about* the Holocaust at all: it is about its own violation, about the disgust and shame it provokes—the shame we feel on reading such uninhibited desecration of what has taken on the aura of a sacral event, and perhaps the poet's own disgust at himself for writing it (it is, after all, his own heart he is toasting, as if to say "It should not be there"). What is stylized here, what we are challenged to transfigure, is not the horror of the "unthinkable fate" but our readiness to assume it is thinkable within the boundaries of our too-human emotional or aesthetic reactions.

Of those reactions, as I have been implying, shame and disgust are the principal ones against which Seidel directs the full furious force of his personality. Adorno anticipates affect theory (or suggests that at least some of its insights are not new) when he invokes the "shame we feel in the presence of the victims." For while Adorno's primary meaning is clearly that we should feel shame that we escaped—that we did not suffer as they did, that we did nothing to prevent their suffering—it would be a mistake to neglect the complexity of shame's multidirectionality. Sedgwick recounts that in her lectures on shame she would ask listeners to imagine what they would feel if a distinctly Seidelean character, "unwashed, half-insane," were to wander "into the lecture hall mumbling loudly, his speech increasingly accusatory and disjointed, and publicly urinate in the front of the room, then wander out again." She pictures "the excruciation" of the onlookers, "each looking down, wishing to be anywhere else yet conscious of the inexorable fate of being exactly there, inside the individual skin of which each was burningly aware; at the same time, though, unable to stanch the hemorrhage of painful identification with the misbehaving man."[92] It is this "double movement" of shame that Seidel rejects: he wants to be the only person in the room not overwhelmed with shame—the urinating intruder, or the homeless man in "To the Muse":

> I watched him squat in the street near the curb while the
>   traffic passed,
> Spreading under himself sheets of newspaper;
>
> Which when he rose he folded neatly
> And carried to the trash basket at the corner.
> Across the street were Mortimer's' outside tables set for lunch.

Seidel refuses not only the commonsense notion of shame, which we feel about our own persons, but the more complex relationality explored by Sedgwick, in which the mere presence of certain others—somehow marked, Sedgwick follows Silvan Tomkins in remarking, by *strangeness*—makes us feel ashamed *for them* or *on their behalf*. It is not only his shame that he challenges, but our own, the shame we feel *for* him as we read his work.

"Mr. Delicious," like so many of Seidel's poems, takes for granted that we are offended, and asks us why we should value our own sensibilities enough to *care* that we are offended. What is it about our *taste* that strikes us as so trustworthy that we should allow it to dictate our *moral* responses? The poem, in other words, is a demonstration of the category mistake that is made when one is *offended* by *evil*. Rather than portray the horror of the Holocaust, or trivialize it (it is already, as received by an infernal culture, trivialized), Seidel instrumentalizes it in order to shame us with our own horror at his violation of decorum. There are aspects of the world that cannot be humanized, cannot be brought to submit to adjudication as matters of taste. Seidel's philosophy, as I read it, is deeply anti-humanistic in its insistence that opinion is beside the point, that a morality of taste is no morality at all. If one is tempted to dismiss Seidel's poetry on grounds of aesthetic taste, in other words, one should at least acknowledge that a central purpose of the poetry is precisely to challenge us to question those grounds.

And if we're disgusted by Seidel's poems, we should at least acknowledge that the poet rouses the affect of disgust exactly to propose a critique of its utility as a moral response. Seidel opposes disgust because it humanizes, makes thinkable, what cannot or should not be humanized:

> Think of the most disgusting thing you can think of.
> It is beautiful in its way.
> It has two legs.
> It has a head of hair.

On one level, these lines make the banal Calvinist argument that the human being is the most disgusting thing imaginable. A reading more attuned to Seidel's critique of a morality of taste will note that the most disgusting thing *imaginable*, in a literal sense—"the most disgusting thing you *can* think of"—has human attributes. Seidel here suggests a limit to the cognitive value of disgust: if the most disgusting thing "is beautiful in its way" *because* we cannot help but see everything as human-shaped, then there are things we cannot see by means of disgust. Disgust is an all too human measure—like cruelty and jealousy in Blake's "A Divine Image," it has a human form. If the horror we seek to confront is instead elided by means of a morality that cannot but humanize what it looks upon—cannot but see itself in what it sees, as though it looked in a mirror—then that morality remains ineluctably *aesthetic*, beautifying what is so monstrous it cannot be assimilated to human systems, which are inexorably grounded in taste.

That disgust should play such a large role in Seidel's critique of a taste-based morality is inevitable. Disgust and taste are intimately linked, perhaps most systematically in Kant, for whom, as Winfried Menninghaus points out, the disgusting extends to "the *morally* disgusting, hence to phenomena subject . . . to an intellectualizing judgment."[93] A different approach to the problem is that taken by Martha Nussbaum, who has recently argued that disgust (and a morality of aesthetic reaction in general) is the wrong basis for criminal legislation, insofar as it represents an attempt to deny our very humanity, a cringing before our embodiment out of a pathological resistance to our own vulnerability.[94] For Seidel, as for Nussbaum, the aesthetics of taste is precisely the field on which the moral cannot possibly be adjudicated, and his provocations call on us to recognize this. It is this morality of taste against which Seidel directs his verse, but with crucial differences. For Seidel, a morality of emotion and aesthetic evaluation is *too* human: the disgusting partakes of its opposite, the beautiful; because it remains within the realm of taste, disgust humanizes the inhuman. On further inspection, though, this contradiction vanishes. What Nussbaum means by *human* is something like what Seidel insists cannot be "humanized": "I like the odor of spoiled meat," Seidel writes of the corpses of the victims of the terrorist attacks of September 11. This odor should not be humanized insofar as that means assimilating it to a symbolic aesthetic order that would tame it, dilute its representation of the ultimate horror at the heart of existence—but in another sense there is nothing more human than this odor, nothing more human than that we are all rotting carcasses. Seidel is trying to make us see what he calls, borrowing the terminology of theoretical physics, "the invisible / Dark matter we are not made of / That I am afraid of"—that which cannot be humanized, about which "opinion" has no bearing.

Seidel, then, seeks to make of himself something not beautiful "in its way," to get at an aspect of self or world that cannot be "humanized." Dark matter, of course, is believed to make up almost all of the universe—the visible matter of insects and stars and cattle cars and Mortimer's and anuses is the merest fraction of what exists. It's a useful trope for Seidel because it is his view of morality writ cosmological. The human image cannot be adequate to the truth, because the truth encompasses horrors that dwarf the human scale. If shame and disgust, reactions based in aesthetic decorum, keep us from seeing the infernal truth about the world—make it into a kind of invisible dark matter—then Seidel will hyperbolically evoke those reactions, as if to demonstrate their inadequacy to the excess that is even more accurate than "the literal standard" established by a morality of taste.

Inferno as literal standard is, as it were, literalized on a Tuesday morning in September, brought abruptly into Seidel's actual home in "The War of the Worlds":

> People on fire are jumping from the eightieth floor
> To flee the fireball.

> In the airplane blind-dating the south tower,
> People are screaming with horror.

> The airplane meeting the north tower
> Erupts with ketchup.

Again we are meant to be offended by the aestheticization of an event that has taken on a sacral aura. The tastelessness required to describe 9/11 in terms of blind dates and ketchup provokes a reaction that Seidel turns against us. The fire is figured as the fake blood ("ketchup") of the television screen, the plane's penetration of the south tower as a blind date, as if the two were contestants on a reality show. The attacks of 9/11 did not simply become a spectacle but were designed to be one, endlessly looped on cable news. But this is a rather obvious interpretation of the poem—even the metaphor of September 11 as reality television is stale by now (Jean Baudrillard apparently having begun work on it by September 12). The violation of decorum is thus built into the event itself, the tastelessness of Seidel's representation diluted by its redundancy.

A more fruitful reading would require us again to attend to the scale of the human. We should note that Seidel once more traffics in the clichés of the outsized event. "9/11" quickly became a kind of emergency code for national trauma, oversaturated with meaning, which is to say all but meaningless for poetry. The attacks themselves are humanized, figured as human actions ("dating," "meeting"). Those familiar with his work cannot but recall the opening of the earlier poem "Spring": "I want to date-rape life," he writes. This line suggests that if we must approach life through the lens of human action, we might at least admit that to do so is to do violence to reality, and that no human violence could possibly be adequate to reality's own. One clue that the redundancy of "The War of the Worlds," too, is deeper than it at first appears is that it erupts onto the surface of the poem *as* redundancy only when the event's human actors take the stage: they are "fleeing the fireball" even though they are already "on fire." In this way, the infernal is perversely humanized, the human figures assuming its fiery aspects in a kind of parody of the way human affects like disgust project, as Blake would have it, the human shape onto everything. Seidel's irony is double: first, his critique of taste's reliance on the human abstract is conducted via the humanization of the planes and the towers. More complexly, the aesthetic defect reproduces the defect of a morality of taste precisely insofar as it *is* a defect. Taste is an aesthetic phenomenon, and the aesthetic is the inevitable horizon of human action. Only a perspective that goes beyond taste is capable of grasping the truly monstrous at the heart of things, the dark matter we are not made of that is not made of us, and in order to go that far, one must *violate* the boundaries established by taste and decorum.

This helps us understand why the Shoah—the *real* Shoah, "terrifying and inadmissible," not the one in books and social studies classes—is a model of the dark matter that taste prevents us from seeing. The Holocaust is a preferred stage for Seidel to defile, because it is a paradigm of an event one is expected to treat with such reverence and respect that its representations are scripted in advance. In the earlier poem "The Complete Works of Anton Webern," the cattle cars of "Mr. Delicious" are already made the vehicles of a poetic violation:

> These trains had kept it all inside.
> These trains had never let their feelings out.
> . . . .
> These trains shat uncontrollably
> All over the sidings and ramps
> Jews for the camps.

Here again, the content of the image is simply grotesque. The trains are personified that they might defecate the Jews onto the ramps—the Jews are not human cows or snow, they're *shit*. This is the more offensive given the well-documented hellish conditions on those trains, whose floors were often covered in feces and quicklime, and many of whose passengers did not survive the journey. That Seidel's Grand Guignol is directed against a moral reliance on taste and decorum is evident from the passage's rhetoric of psychobabble and self-help psychology, whose spokespersons urge us not to "keep it all inside," to let our feelings out rather than hold them in. Seidel follows this advice, and shits his feelings all over his readers: you think *feelings* are what matter, I'll show you feelings.

The Holocaust presents an especial affront to attempts to transcend feeling. Like a beautiful woman's anus, the Holocaust should not be there. *Seidel* certainly wasn't there:

> I don't want to remember the Holocaust.
> I'm *thick* of remembering the Holocaust.
> To the best of my ability, I wasn't there anyway.

This refuses the logic of "never forget," but with characteristic perversity, as though Seidel took the injunction personally. The tastelessness is prominent as usual: what Seidel *wants* can hardly be at issue, while the childishness of saying you're "sick" of remembering the Shoah is matched only by the inappropriately comic affectation of a child's lisp. But what is at issue in the call to remember something you didn't experience? Can it be that the very insistence on remembering prevents us from seeing, that the memorialization of the event domesticates it, brings it down to a manageably human scale, makes us too "thick" to penetrate its horror?

It is difficult to determine Seidel's position on the question of whether the Holocaust is essentially continuous with human action or constitutes a radical rupture. Certainly the Sadean-Nietzschean thrust of his critique would seem to indicate agreement with the tenor (if not the political tendency) of Adorno and Horkheimer's view that barbarism is constitutive of modernity as such, and the possibility of civilizational rupture inheres in the very fabric of instrumental rationality. But this is countered by the poems' repeated insistence that the human is not commensurate to the scale of evil represented by the Holocaust. "To the best of my ability, I wasn't there anyway" is a very strange line. His not having been there has nothing to do with his "ability"—he was a nine-year-old boy in St. Louis when the war ended, the son of a wealthy coal magnate. Is the absurdity of claiming agency for contingent historical circumstance intended as a rebuke to those who would locate the Holocaust within the continuum of human action?

Regardless of whether Seidel goes so far as this, he is certainly concerned with the extent to which the diabolical conditions of modernity nullify human agency, and the second of his urgent tasks as a poet, coexisting uneasily with the moral critique, is to stake out a position from which agency might be recovered. This would also produce an expansion of agency, a new freedom and strength for the self: "I felt invulnerable, without feelings, without pores." He seeks an ideology of self-representation that might be adequate to an infernal present—and such an ideology has no room for delicacy of feeling, or indeed for the porosity of feeling that encourages us to let our feelings out, not to hold them in. Seeking to free himself from the tyranny of feeling, Seidel spews his feelings on the page, refusing to curb their intensity—by giving them free rein, he both parodies the logic of the self-help movement and purges himself. It is important to note that this intensified self-presence is directed against taste, but for a very different reason than that which motivates Seidel's critique of a morality blinded to the truth of the world. Seidel's aggressive claim of agency is related to—in fact, reliant on—the horror he diagnoses, and the two currents of his poetry share a vehicle in his offensive against taste.

For Seidel is responding to this infernal present when he presents himself as infernal. He represents the self not as a bulwark against a ruined culture, or as merely determined by it, but as appropriate to it—he makes himself into a devil in order to be at home in hell.* If our sensibilities enrage him, it is not because our feelings of horror and umbrage seek to deny that we too belong to the infernal but because they prevent us from seeing it in the first place. To perceive a morality of taste as a veneer is not incompatible with a moral sense of another kind. Seidel's outrageousness is incomprehensible without a recognition that he is outraged, that he would not have to try to make a home in hell if he felt at home there already—or if he could believe that there were an alternative to life in hell, the possibility of salvation through the expiation of sins rather than the negative salvation of their embrace.

In "December," Seidel imagines 9/11 as an infernal parody of the Eucharist, a sacrament dedicated to the proposition that salvation depends on external agency: "I like the color of the smell. I like the odor of spoiled meat. / I like how gangrene transubstantiates warm firm flesh into rotten sleet."

We are close to Sade here, whose novels often stage blasphemous travesties of Catholic rites. Like Sade, Seidel seems to risk lapsing into mere antinomianism, "liking" what disgusts us, transported into synesthesiac ecstasy by the smell of rotten human flesh. As the Jews become human snow, the victims of 9/11 become dirty sleet—the profundity of carnage reduced to a weather report. But the imagery recalls us to Seidel's preoccupation with his own mortality, to the always unwelcome recognition that we are only dying animals, organic systems of reproduction and waste excretion whose hearts, on their sticks, will be quite consumed away. In *The Cosmos Poems*, Seidel repeatedly stresses our relative insignificance within

---

* Perhaps it is worth pointing out that *devil*, from *diaballein*, and *hyperbole*, from *hyperballein*, share an etymology—*ballein*, to throw. The diabolical is cast out, while the hyperbolic is thrown too far.

the immensity of the universe, of whose nature we remain almost wholly ignorant (the invisible dark matter we are not made of apparently making up most of everything that is). The similarity to Nietzsche's naturalistic perspective is not accidental, Nietzsche who wrote of "a star on which clever animals invented knowledge" and knew that our knowledge and belief systems and values would soon be snuffed out:

> After nature had drawn a few breaths, the star grew cold, and the clever animals had to die. . . . [The intellect] was given only as an aid to the most unfortunate, most delicate, most evanescent beings in order to hold them for a minute in existence, from which otherwise, without this gift, they would have every reason to flee . . .

Seidel elaborates this view of a universe governed by "the tendency / Not to be." "Death is all there is," he quips, revising the Beatles: "Death will have to do." "What, indeed, does man know of himself!" Nietzsche continues; what indeed do we know of the dark matter we are, of which we are not made. Like Seidel, Nietzsche insisted that we are deceiving ourselves, that we are no more than "clever animals" that will become "spoiled meat." We shy from the truths our bodies, those total nightmares, would tell us, and insist that the anus "should not be there":

> Does not nature keep much the most from him, even about his body, to spellbind and confine him in a proud, deceptive consciousness, far from the coils of the intestines, the quick current of the bloodstream, and the involved tremors of the fibers?[95]

Thus the irony of a humanizing perspective: for Nussbaum, the human *is* "the coils of the intestines," while what Seidel has in mind is "beautiful in its way" precisely because it fantasizes that the human is noble and fair.

Seidel turns these coils and tremors into sources of power and delight—the foundations of a hypertrophied self-presence—by embracing the Nietzschean *amor fati*. "I like" that we are bags of rotting meat, "I like" the people on fire jumping from the eightieth floor, "I like" the carbon ash of human corpses drifting like an early snow onto the streets of downtown Manhattan. This bears more than superficial resemblance to Nietzsche's recommendation of "an unreserved yea-saying even to suffering, even to guilt, even to everything questionable and strange about existence"—although Seidel is more likely to say "no" to guilt by embracing those actions that from a conventional moral standpoint should produce guilt.[96]

The impetus for such relentless assertion of the self is in part the overriding suspicion that as the appendage of an infernal culture, the self is nothing, that "we are not made of" anything. "*I* isn't anything," Seidel writes in "Barbados": "And *I* is the first one hacked to pieces." If the self isn't anything—not even part of "the nothing" "we know so much" of—then what could its taste possibly amount to? This is the critique of the metaphysics of presence applied to the real world, where the self is a dispersed network not of signifiers but of body parts on the jungle floor. The death drive is figured here as the desire to literalize the trope of the subject's dispersal: the paradoxical desire "to cut oneself in two" because one suspects one's self is nothing.

But an alternative is to hold that if the self is nothing, one might as well behave as if it were everything. In "Barbados," therefore, we meet Seidel as a tourist staying at "[l]iterally the most expensive hotel in the world" in a tropical paradise built on the slave trade, which he envisions as a surreal cartoon:

> The most expensive hotel in the world
> Is the slave ship unloading Africans on the moon.
> They wear the opposite of space suits floating off the dock
> To a sugar mill on a hilltop.
> They float into the machinery.

A slave's arm gets caught in the machine, which "isn't vegetarian," and "turns into brown sugar." The slave's "screams can't be heard above the roar."

It isn't the lack of a moralizing perspective on slavery that is offensive (as if we needed Seidel to remind us that slavery is bad) but the sense that the poet is simply gloating over the human costs that prop up his privilege—that he is not just refusing to denounce the fruits of slavery but actively enjoying them *as such*. Another poet might write a poem that acknowledges that his island vacation was made possible by the exploitation of other humans, in order to explore the complex relations of the self's dedication to its pleasures with the guilt induced by those pleasures' price. But Seidel gives the impression that he is simply using an atrocity, and another representationally exhausted one at that, to expand his sense of himself—as if all the evil of slavery were worthwhile if it produced one afternoon in Frederick Seidel's life of "pure aristo privilege." The machinery of the world—nature, politics, economy—eats the "spoiled meat" of human beings, grinds it up and spits it out, despite the refined vegetarian taste of liberal sensibilities. Hacking the "I" to pieces is just what the world does. A single slave's screams cannot be heard above the roar of the "epileptic fit" of the universe. So what would Seidel's denying himself his tastes accomplish, compared with the aggrandizement of self-power that they enable?

For Seidel's denunciation of taste as a moral category is perversely dependent on his affirmation of his own exquisite taste in luxury items. This millionaire poet has never had to work for a living, and his poems rarely fail to evince this. He represents himself unapologetically as a man of wealth and taste. Many readers will find this dimension of his poems the most vulgar of all. Seidel stays, of course, at "[l]iterally the most expensive hotel in the world," smugly poeticized as "the smell of rain about to fall." (The intertext here is offensive in itself—from his playboy paradise, Seidel is paraphrasing lines Pound wrote in the death cells about "the clouds

over Taishan / When some of the rain has fallen / and half remains
yet to fall."[97]) His collected poems rub their readers' noses in Seidel's
appetite for expensive things: Cartier watches, his Savile Row tai-
lor; there are paeans to the famous jeweler Joel Rosenthal. But for
Seidel's most conspicuous consumption, we must turn to the poems
about his six-figure custom-made Ducati motorcycles. He is especially fond of the Ducati 916, "the most beautiful motorcycle ever
made," an aesthetic "miracle / Which ought to be in the Museum of
Modern Art." He flies to Bologna to see his bike being built; he is
shepherded through security; it is like being initiated into religious
mysteries:

> The Lord is my shepherd and the Director of Superbike Racing.
> He buzzes me through three layers of security
> To the innermost secret sanctum of the racing department
> . . . .
> Trains are delayed.
> The Florence sky is falling snow.

The trains and snow are innocent here, within this temple of exquisite taste, but we are still disgusted. How crass is this profligacy,
how worshipful an ostentation. In passages like this, Seidel is still
challenging our dependency on cultivated liberal taste, no less aesthetic than his literal commodity fetishism. But these moments are
also distasteful because they are so blatantly hypocritical: he sneers at
our disgust and horror, our commitment to aesthetic propriety, and
then he kneels before the "altar" on which his beloved superbikes
are consecrated.

* * *

The one time a cognate of the word *shame* appears in Seidel's omni-
bus *Poems 1959–2009* is in the last line of a poem from *Evening Man*.

Seidel is describing a friend's husband whose sudden partial paralysis puzzles his doctors:

> It is exactly as if he'd had a stroke—though he is young.
> But his speech and cognition are unimpaired.
> But he can't even use a bedpan or sit up in bed.
> Art throws the dog a bone.
> I am ashamed of my poem.

Here Seidel acknowledges the impropriety of turning a friend's trauma into the occasion for a poem, but of course his insincerity is almost audible. He's about as ashamed as Sidney's Astrophil in Sonnet 34: "Art not asham'd to publish thy disease? / Nay, that may breed my fame, it is so rare." Much more suggestive is the penultimate line, which recalls Elizabeth Bishop's famous rebuke of Robert Lowell after he incorporated passages from Elizabeth Hardwick's letters into the poems of *The Dolphin*: "Art just isn't worth that much."[98] The dog—surely Seidel himself in this case—is the paragon of shamelessness, as Raymond Geuss has pointed out:

> The dog . . . ignores human social conventions and is completely free of any form of shame. From the dog the followers of Diogenes acquired their name: Cynics. Complete shamelessness—learning to ignore others' negative reactions of disgust at one's appearance and behavior—is the only true road to the self-sufficiency that is the distinguishing characteristic of the good human life.

In one sense, Seidel more closely resembles the Cynics' "precursor and patron saint" Herakles than he does Diogenes: "Herakles made no attempt to reduce his needs and desires. He was, on the contrary, notorious for his crude and unbridled passions . . ." But Herakles was also noted for his altruism. Like Diogenes and his followers, Seidel adopts "the goal of self-sufficiency without the altruism." This is, as Geuss notes, "deeply unpolitical":

> First, by aspiring to complete self-sufficiency one tries to remove oneself from the state of mutual dependence on other humans, which is one of the basic preconditions of politics. Second, to assume an attitude of complete indifference to others' opinions, and especially to behave in ways one knows others will find disgusting, is consciously to produce in others the experience of a barrier and tacitly to give them to understand that one expects to be able to do without their assistance, an assumption they might, justifiably or not, find insulting.[99]

Of course, Seidel is not "behaving" in these ways, but *representing* himself as disgusting and indifferent to others' opinions. His claim that the poems are to be taken at face value might also be understood, then, as a kind of speech act meant to ensure that the representations have the force of disgusting conduct. In other words, Seidel's shamelessness is a form of self-sufficiency, an extreme assertion of a self that delights and affrights in the infernal, that in fact *requires* the infernal as the only tableau adequate to the force of the personality on display. Anything less than hell itself would be crowded out by Seidel's hyperbole, which would then seem disproportionate to its conditions. In "December," he announces: "Down here in hell we do don't. / I can't think of anything I won't."

We're in hell, but we still "do don't." *Don't* is what we do do: don't look at the anus, don't instrumentalize the Holocaust, don't flash your privilege. Power and freedom inhere in the violation of prohibitions, as Sade knew, and Sade could have said, "I can't think of anything I won't." Even to declare this much is to declare that one accepts no limits to agency, that one's will is the only law one recognizes. In practice this is disastrous, but as a poetic strategy predicated on the violation of taboos that govern acceptable discourse, it offers a neat solution to the perceived impotence of individual will in our modern hells, where it can seem that all we are able to do is *don't*.

Seidel elaborates this position in "The Tenth Month": "Someone is wagging a finger in her face—*Charlotte! / Down here in hell we don't do that! /* As if she were a child." An adult would recognize the absurdity of schoolmarmishly lecturing someone about her bad behavior in hell, and would find such proscriptions childish. But down here in hell we relish issuing prohibitions, as if by allowing disgust to guide us, by curbing our excess and waste, we could regulate horror out of view, as in "Home":

> I bend down with a bag to clean up after the dog.
> I take the shit out of the bag
> And stuff it back up inside the dog
>
> And sew the anus closed.

But it is in the very violation of prohibition—letting shit happen—that Seidel differentiates himself from the other damned souls, at least within the poetic sphere: "I can't think of anything I won't" do (or think or write or say or even prohibit). To accept any limit would imply that there are some actions (or thoughts or words) worth being ashamed of. The line "I am ashamed of my poem," then, is just more proof of Seidel's shamelessness: he can't think of anything he won't write, including that. To elevate any commitment—even one to shamelessness—to the status of a principle by which to live would be to limit the potential scope of agency. Seidel's singular poetic achievement is to have made the rejection of taste the pivot on which turn both the disclosure of radical evil and the only means of self-assertion in its flames.

But there is an instability at the heart of Seidel's poetics. The twin motives of his poems—to render and face real evil and to carve out within that reality a space of power and agency for the self—are ultimately incompatible with each other. This, I feel, is the source of the strange appeal of Seidel's poetry. For if the point of the offense, the tastelessness, the excess, is to make us see that our offense, our taste, our timidity *do not matter*, that they leave evil untouched, that they allow it to flourish, then the desideratum must be that we should *cease to be offended*, should give up our reliance on a morality of taste. But if we did that then the second motive, the motive of agency, would fail. For if we saw the conditions of modernity as the hell they are, flensed of our illusions of taste, Seidel's personality would no longer appear as a grotesque hyperbole but as entirely adequate to his surroundings. All *other* poets would then seem cowardly devotees of litotes. Seidel's poetic voice can retain its force only if readers perceive it as a violation of, rather than as the only appropriate response to, the demands of decorum.

EQUIPMENT FOR SINKING

> Looks like what drives me crazy
> Don't have no effect on you—
> But I'm gonna keep on at it
> Till it drives you crazy, too.

This little poem by Langston Hughes comes back to me too often. Someone shoots up a church. The cops leave another black body in the street. Rain forests burn. Someone shoots up an elementary school. Workers jump from an Apple factory in China. CEOs make in an hour what their employees earn in a year. Someone shoots up a movie theater. American drone bombs obliterate a wedding party. Half of marine life disappears.

I know: You've heard it all before. I've heard it all before too. We've all heard it all before: we don't hear it anymore. And anyway, what can we do?

There is no limit to what a poem can't do.

* * *

Poetry makes nothing happen—everyone knows that. Nothing is what poetry can do, and it does it. What drives Hughes crazy—the lynching tree, the landlord, the "mint / Of blood and sorrow," America that never yet has been America—makes nothing happen. "Go *slow*," would-be allies counsel, "While the bite / Of the dog is fast."

I'm gonna keep on at it—
That's the only way nothing won't happen.

* * *

Hughes's little poem "Evil" appeared in his collection *Shakespeare in Harlem* in 1942. The reviewer for the *Times* wrote that "it looks at the moment as if the richest Negro minds had not gone into literature."

Poetry makes all sorts of things happen. This book has been about some of them.

What doesn't happen happens no place; it happens in utopia.

> From this the poem springs: that we live in a place
> That is not our own and, much more, not ourselves
> And hard it is in spite of blazoned days.

I believe Wallace Stevens. I believe that poetry springs from lack, from a recognition or sense that the world's not ours, not us, not easy.

* * *

Or one might speak in Marxian terms, like Adorno, of the contradiction between what the forces of production could bring about—"a condition worthy of human beings," "a paradise on earth"—and what the relations of production actually generate: "wrong life," "an existence outrageously unlovely."[100]

Sometimes I walk down Wall Street just to feel fury, to remind myself what the real dregs of humanity look like. They look good.

* * *

There are many ways of convicting everything of not being some-thing else. This is what art is *for*. In spite of blazoned days.

* * *

A commercial for the Honda Civic begins with a cod blues band playing a song on a porch: "Today is pretty bad / Today the world is pretty sad." The proof flashes on the screen: crashing markets, collapsing ice shelves, foreclosed homes, laid-off workers, billowing pollution, riot cops, trash dunes. "Yeah it's worse than ever / But that's just where we're at."

Cut to an attractive young woman driving a new Civic: "Except, it's not." Other fresh, multicultural faces join in: "It isn't." "It really just ain't." "Today is pretty great."

"This world's full of problems," the soulful singer protests, but now we've got this killjoy's number. The fresh faces fling rebuttals: "What about science?" "Selfies?" "Puppies?" "What about being ac-cepted for who you are?"

The Civic asseveration concludes with a chorus of "Today is pretty great!"

When ideology is this transparent—forced to acknowledge the objective state of things before staging its refutation—you know things are bad.

* * *

In spite of blazoned days. Yeats can't manage a half hour, much less a day, but his evocation of transient bliss is as convincing as any I know:

> While on the shop and street I gazed
> My body of a sudden blazed;
> And twenty minutes more or less

> It seemed, so great my happiness,
> That I was blessed and could bless.

This is convincing precisely because limited, "hemmed in," Oren Izenberg writes, "by a duration that is comically precise and approximate at once."

Izenberg asks whether there might exist a "poetry of ease":

> poetry that does not speak of that state as one speaks of an unknown country we might wish one day to visit—Cockaigne, Bensalem, Innisfree—but rather a poetry that expresses ease as we express our native air: stirring it with our living presence, not exhausting it with our efforts.[101]

Is there a poetry of blessedness and blessing within human time but without one eye on the clock, a poem that springs from the opposite of the condition Stevens describes? A hymn to a place that is *ourselves*—a unity of habitation and self?

I guess I wonder why anyone in a state of ease would bother to write a poem.

* * *

Adorno was much taken with "Hegel's statement in his *Aesthetics* that as long as there is an awareness of suffering among human beings there must also be art as the objective form of that awareness."[102] This awareness need not be the paraphrasable matter of the work—there are innumerable odes to joy and parties in the USA.

Kenneth Burke: "form, a public matter that symbolically enrolls us with allies who will share the burdens with us."

* * *

A high school kid calls in a request to an Indiana radio station as a kegger winds down in 1983:

> I'm up here in Muncie, and a friend of mine just passed away, and, uh, I wanted to know if you'd play Bob Seger, 'Against the Wind,' and dedicate it to Tim Barton. Could you do that for me? Tim Barton? He had a car wreck, and, uh, he got hit broadside, and it made his little Pinto about two foot wide. And, you know, he was in a coma since Friday, and he just passed away today, and I was wondering if you'd, you know, play that for us.

This is a scene from Joel DeMott and Jeff Kreines's Wisemanesque documentary *Seventeen*, about working-class high school youth in the Rust Belt, which PBS refused to air: the kids' cussing, drinking, pot smoking, and interracial dating scared corporate sponsor Xerox.

The DJ does play Seger's cheesy, glorious ballad, and the few kids who haven't gone home or passed out gather to listen to it in a bedroom with faux wood paneling. The camera focuses on the boy who placed the call, then on two girls slumped side by side on the bed. They look at the floor, look inside themselves, and sing along, but silently, their lips moving as if they were whispering a prayer for their dead friend. They wipe tears from their eyes. The mother of one of the girls looks on from the door, half in shadow. She wipes her own tears away and fades from the shot.

Seems like yesterday.

* * *

The sons and daughters of American wood paneling needed Bob Seger then, as I suppose today they need One Republic or Sam Hunt.

"Against the Wind" was a staple on the tape deck of my dad's

Subaru in the early '80s. It's a ruthlessly tasteful song, not a lick out of place, mixed to within an inch of guest hairstylist Glenn Frey's stock options. It lacks the bushy contours of Seger's best numbers ("Night Moves," "Back in '72," and "Roll Me Away," for the record), which know exactly how full of shit they are. Despite one great line ("Wish I didn't know now what I didn't know then"), "Against the Wind" is trope-by-committee, earnest as an HR rep.

But sometimes that's what you want—generic, sanded-down professionalism, an oiled star-maker machine grand enough to grind a two-foot-wide Pinto into powder.

* * *

Except for a brief phase in high school when I scoffed at any band bigger than Camper Van Beethoven (which at my high school meant U2 and the Grateful Dead), the viral marketability of the music I love has never bothered me much.

I had the good fortune to become obsessed with the radio in 1983, an annus mirabilis for pop: "Billie Jean," "Down Under," "Burning Down the House," "Every Breath You Take," "Little Red Corvette," "True," "Holiday," "Der Kommissar," "Back on the Chain Gang," "Faithfully," "Africa," "Rock the Casbah," "Twilight Zone," "Lawyers in Love," "Our House," "Photograph," "Cum on Feel the Noize," "Always Something There to Remind Me," "Sweet Dreams," "(Keep Feeling) Fascination," "Electric Avenue." I knew them all by heart. The next year would bring "Oh Sherrie," "Jump," "Run Runaway," "What's Love Got to Do with It," "When Doves Cry," "Dancing in the Dark," "We're Not Gonna Take It," "Missing You," and more.

Bliss was it in that dawn to do as you were told and listen to the radio.

* * *

Mass-produced, standardized pop is designed to reinforce the social order, despite appearances to the contrary. It mimics the relentless cycle of everyday life: verse-chorus-ideology of economic domination-verse.

So have I heard, and do in part believe it.

This process is mysterious, but one of its corollaries is transparent. We're used to reading that Taylor Swift just purchased Ghana or whatever. No other art I love so directly reproduces the barbarism of economic injustice.

But I take it on faith that popular music *is* art (I take a great many things about art on faith, and so do you), for all its evanescence and monetization. And art is bidirectional, dialectical, contradictory. Its form points toward the brightly burning Dumpster we have made of the world—toward the swindle, the sales copy—but *therefore* also toward a world of never-ending happiness, where you can always see the sun, day or night.

* * *

Maybe it's just me.

I have friends to whom art seems to arise from all kinds of impulses, to whom today seems *pretty great*—full of the usual horrors, sure, but very far from terminal, full as well of promise and hope.

Even that stupid commercial points beyond itself, to a dissatisfaction with the structure of the *pretty great* world—how great can it really be as long as you're not driving the new Honda Civic?

I believe, with the usual suspects, that art exposes the contradictions of the present dispensation and thus preserves the yearning for the *other*, better world that can be achieved only by negating the existing one.

It says nothing about the forms that world might take. It says nothing about the likelihood of achieving it.

* * *

In a poem called "(It was raining in das Kapital)," Joshua Clover writes, "We thought it was 1900 / but it was MCM again," extending the pun of the title into history itself, time as capital. Marxian transformations, fiscal years. 1900—eve of the twentieth century, ten years before the modernist rupture, when "human character changed," according to Virginia Woolf—is transformed into Roman numerals, familiar from film copyright notices, which the prime symbol then transforms into Marx's general formula for capital, "the unceasing movement of profit-making": money (M) into commodities (C) back into money, "the original sum advanced, plus an increment . . . I call 'surplus-value'" (M').

The formal changes represented by 1900 shift duck-rabbit-like into the fundamental change of form that governs our lives, capital—a process, not a thing, "structure in motion" as Clover puts it elsewhere. "Why do things / seem to shudder / because volatility."

It's not 1900 again, but 1900-prime—the volatility of the modern once again intervening in the volatility of capital, but with an added increment, a chance to learn from and make good on the broken, bloody promises of the twentieth century. Elsewhere, Clover poeticizes the ritual de-Stalinization the left must ceaselessly perform: "The longest social experiment in history / Has been abandoned, nobody liked it anyway, the cigarettes were awful." The experiment in question is of course Soviet communism, which "Stalin's beard ruined . . . for everyone." Clover dreams of a revolution with better cigarettes and "Marc Jacobins" "walking / With headphones on through the theory district."

At this point in history, the responsible critic declares, such hopes seem delusional, even dangerous. Everybody knows that liberal capitalist democracy is the final costume Spirit will don. But as Clover reminds us, "history isn't something."

"History *does* nothing," Marx and Engels write in *The Holy Family*, against the idealist conception of history, "it 'possesses *no* immense wealth,' it 'wages *no* battles.' It is *man*, real, living man who does all that, who possesses and fights; 'history' is not, as it were, a person apart, using man as a means to achieve *its own* aims; history is *nothing but* the activity of man pursuing his aims."

History makes nothing happen.

* * *

"How high that highest candle lights the dark," says Stevens (whose work is rarely as ahistorical as it seems) of the imagination. I love Stevens, forever addressing some bird he doesn't like.

But Gwendolyn Brooks, hymning the rioters in Chicago after the murder of Martin Luther King Jr., is the poet I return to to think about the something that history isn't and the nothing it is:

>   what
> is going on
> is going on.
> Fire.
> That is their way of lighting candles in the darkness.

* * *

"The poem must be on the side of riots looting barricades occupations manifestos communes slogans fire and enemies," Clover says.

This is directed, of course, against the tradition of disinterestedness in which the poem must be a free and autonomous end in itself. And while I'm not sure that anyone really believes art is autonomous in any strict sense, the claim is made often enough to be worth the rebuttal.

As Clover put it to me, "The presupposition that all ideas must serve 'poetry' and indeed may have been contrived so as to make the 'poetry' work seems odd to me." He counters that "commitments might come first, and that 'poetry' might be a particular way to work through" these commitments.

Aesthetic life is a sphere of self-directed activity whose external ramifications, despite periodic utopian exuberances, are minimal at best. Clover imagines the poem not as a direct intervention in history but as a site for *working through* commitments, questions, problems.

Like Clover, his labelmate Juliana Spahr, in her collection *That Winter the Wolf Came*, lights up what's going on—which, whether you face it or not, is going on. For me, at this moment, she and Clover best represent how art confronts its own quixotism and extravagance. The concrete situation out of which their poems, and everything else in the world, arise is that capital is killing us. These are poems about and for the riots goin' on, the riots yet to come. They are hopeful-skeptical, sorry-grateful.

The Occupy Oakland movement is figured in Spahr's work as a lover named "Non-Revolution"—"such a minor uprising," it did not issue in Revolution, "an entirely different lover, one I was not sure I was ready for and yet longed for so much"—within whose remembered arms these verse essays connect the fluctuations of Brent crude to the flight paths of brent geese; breast milk to a Whitmanian catalog of "brominated fire retardants of Koppers Ind." and "water/ oil repellent paper coating of 3M"; nature to second nature; police kettling to texted heart emoticons; NSA to FTP; the beginning of a song to "the singer crying on the bathroom floor"; "what is being lost" to "I begin walking, determined, head down."

The last poem in the book, "Turnt," says yes to no, to occupation and riot; says yes to the velocities of change in "the depths of friends":

> I was at the poetry reading and Mia didn't go. She was
>   supposed to read too but she didn't. She said she wanted
>   to see what happens. Then she texts I love you and I
>   know then that Trader Joe's has been looted. All the
>   wines out in the street.
> Such sweet elixir, FOMO.
> . . . .
>   The march continues on, Nathan continues on, turns
>   left a block away and then when Nathan texts me back I

know the Whole Foods is looted and they are all drinking
champagne, dancing. All of them will get a cold later.
Riot champagne becomes a term among us that winter.
I wasn't there but I was there too. My germs were there.
I too had that cold.

We have heard this syntax before:

> I too felt the curious abrupt questionings stir within
> me,
> In the day among crowds of people sometimes they
> came upon me,
> In my walks home late at night or as I lay in my
> bed they came upon me,

> I too had been struck from the float forever held in
> solution,
> I too had receiv'd identity by my body,
> That I was, I knew was of my body, and what I
> should be, I knew I should be of my body.

Whitman's democratic ode to the East River ferry passengers
is transplanted to the opposite coast and "turnt" into "a movement
poem" by Spahr. Whitman opens at sunset—"Clouds of the west—
sun there half an hour high—I see you also face to face"—while
Spahr marches at "rosy fingered dusk." The epithet reminds me that
Allen Grossman called Whitman's "face to face" a Homeric "signifier of heroic encounter." "Is this poem too heroic?" Spahr asks.
"I worry it is. / Or I know it is." Whitman's "crowds of men and
women attired in the usual costumes" take on a different charge as
Spahr's anti-capitalist demonstrators, who don masks to prevent
identification by the police and to protect themselves from tear gas:
"At first we didn't mask up. We were poets. / Then slowly one by
one we did."

"We were poets"—therefore harmless, our private and ineffectual activity cordoned off from the realm where things go down, where heads get busted. But poets have often worn masks, from the Greek chorus to Pessoa, to Whitman himself, concealing "the real me," "the me myself," behind his "arrogant poems."

Both poems eulogize the loss of individuation a mask enables, the slipping out of the self into something larger, into the crowd, the current, into the mystic:

> The impalpable sustenance of me from all things, at
>   all hours of the day,
> The simple, compact, well-join'd scheme, myself
>   disintegrated, every one disintegrated yet part
>   of the scheme,
> The similitudes of the past and those of the future,
> The glories strung like beads on my smallest sights
>   and hearings, on the walk in the street, and
>   the passage over the river,
> The current rushing so swiftly and swimming with
>   me far away,
> The others that are to follow me, the ties between me
>   and them,
> The certainty of others—the life, love, sight, hear-
>   ing of others.

The waves of "Turnt" are metaphorical, and the ties between Spahr and others are more explicit, ties of political dedication, danger, and drive:

> At that moment, I melted my body into it and it embraced
>   me.
> Rosy fingered dusk and all that.
> Come here, it sang, listen.
> And then I was borne along by the waves all night and the

> whirlpool, the fig tree, and I was the bat, hanging on
> patiently.

"It" is the march, the demonstration, the uprising, the movement, which Spahr tropes as a living thing, with its own voice, its own nervous system. It is both Charybdis and the fig tree Odysseus clings to like a bat, monster and lifeline. Spahr is in love with "it," she tallies its glories strung along her sight and hearing. Melting her body into it, she receives identity.*

So much FOMO, that sweet elixir, Spahr's poems give me.

Because above all else Spahr's experience of this non-revolution, this movement, this *it*—is one of *joy*. "You can hear it sometimes. It often has a soundtrack. Sometimes it has drums and brass. Sometimes just joy. . . . A group of women walk by the car and stop to take photographs. So much joy they have. They are laughing with such triumph. Selfies and all. Turnt."

I think of Craig Finn's introduction to "Killer Parties" on the Hold Steady's live album *A Positive Rage*: "There is *so much joy* in what we do up here! I want to thank you for being here to share that joy with us."

Right, it's corny. But when Spahr writes, in a prose poem, of falling for Non-Revolution in the "certainty of others, the life, love, sight, hearing of others"—

> I had no control. When I wondered it, wondered how it could
> be like this for me at this moment, I blamed it on the art. For

---

* Michael Clune helpfully suggested to me that Elias Canetti's *Crowds and Power* might ground Spahr's implication that crowds can legitimize, through collective experience, a celebration of emotion that might otherwise be stigmatized as bourgeois. More germane for my purposes is E. P. Thompson's magnificent essay "The Moral Economy of the English Crowd in the Eighteenth Century."

all the art I have ever loved has been for whatever it is that Non-Revolution was suggesting it could possibly be. For the river running backwards. For the wind and the rain. And I am someone who loves art, who has always loved art, despite. Despite its institutions and its patronages and its nationalisms and its capitalisms. All the art that has had a crowd scene in it in which the crowd has been loved, I have loved.

—I see the big rooms pop music happens in night after night, in which the crowd is loved, in which love is big and crowded and possible, despite. And then Spahr, recounting a conversation with a friend who took part in an earlier non-revolutionary uprising, makes the connection explicit: "She knows something, how this being with can be easily described with the private emotions of love and desire, the same emotions that are pillaged and packaged in popular music."

Non-Revolution, like pop, points beyond itself. What Spahr loves art "for" is whatever Non-Revolution was suggesting it could be—revolution, surely. But a revolution that sounds a lot like a poem: the river running backwards recalls the opening of the ninth book of *The Prelude*, in which Wordsworth records his ambivalent response to the French Revolution.

But "eventually Non-Revolution and me were over," and Spahr recollects her ex in non-tranquility, emotion pouring from her like a jukebox. She stands "on the corner for a few minutes feeling lost, with a funny almost choking expression on my face." (The dark threw its patches down upon Whitman also.)

My friend looks at me and she says what is wrong with you? and I say nothing, I'm just confused. And then she says I was worried you were choking; you had a funny expression. It's like that. A sort of choking. A staring off into space that often precedes a coughing-choking. The it of it's all fucked; it's all good. The depression that follows after the most mundane of uprisings is over. Life feels less. And might for a long time. It might be years before a day will go by that I do not think about Non-Revolution.

Jilted by her lover, Spahr, like her friend, turns to pop's packaged emotions. Behind these lines I hear pop stars from Everett Sloane to Burt Bacharach to Stephen Sondheim to Pablo Neruda to Carole King to Naked Eyes to Frank Ocean. And you start to think, if a failed revolution can be a lover, can a poem be a pop song?

Critics writing about poetry usually assume, without thinking about it, that the poem has priority. Izenberg has challenged this assumption: "The *a priori* conviction that all poetic projects imagine the crucial relation to poetry to be a relation to an object—an object of labor, of perception, of interpretation—is an unwarranted assumption, even a sort of fetishism." He insists that "what the poet intends by means of poetry is not always the poem." Commitments might come first—political, as in Clover's and Spahr's cases, or ontological, or what have you.

I'm interested in the markers of this priority. I take it that a kind of naïveté, whether actual or imputed—one reviewer writes that she "wondered if [Clover is] for real"—can be one such sign. Keston Sutherland calls this naïveté "the indigenous stupidity of poets" who "want more than can be intelligently wanted"; for Izenberg, such poets are "outscale desirers," articulating "forms of wanting or willing unbound from ordinary calculations of plausibility or even possibility."

Spahr and Clover are aware that their projects (which, politically and poetically, I admire and support) will strike some as desperate attempts to recapture *l'esprit de soixante-huit*: "There will be a revolution or there will not," Clover writes. "If the latter these poems were nothing but entertainments. If the former it will succeed or fail. If the latter these poems were better than nothing."

Poetry like this—in its outscale desire, its extravagant want, its implausible or impossible will—thus risks the embarrassment of overshooting the target, aiming for the negation of the social order and hitting "better than nothing," the very lesser-evil reformist logic it riotously rejects.

I find these embarrassments isomorphic with the more famil-iar extravagances of pop music*—big, throbbing, teenage emotions. Both are utopian (the latter in spite of itself), charged with an excess that throws into relief the "insufficiently meaningful world" (Guy Debord). Swim out past the breakers, watch the world die.

* * *

I've been suggesting that this is how *all* poetry works. So that explic-itly commitment-first poetry is merely a special case that lights the dark of a generally implicit utopianism. Thus, as long as we fall back to this world, all poetry is bathos—the fine art of sinking.†

"Can a poem be a pop song?" is my dumbed-down version of Allen Grossman's bewilderment before the mystery of what poetry "can *now mean* in the context of the actual human task. What obliga-tions 'poetry' requires. What benefit to the human world the obliga-tion, privilege, or competence named 'poetry'—*the vocation to 'poetic work'*—implies or promises."[103]

* * *

Clover suggests a riot can be pop music:

> Once fire is the form of the spectacle the problem
> becomes how to set fire to fire.
> Some friends were prepared to help with this which

---

* I owe this formulation to Anahid Nersessian.

† I owe this Popean formulation to Oren Izenberg.

Michael Jackson having died and then Whitney Houston was the new pop music.

Poetry and pop music and riots produce the same upswelling, the "certainty of others, the life, love, sight, hearing of others," enrolling us with allies who will share the burdens with us, a crowd that is loved.

But only the last of these might conceivably produce a change in the structure of things, which would perforce put an end to the first two. At least as we know them.

PLAYLIST

Paige Ackerson-Kiely
"Misery Trail" (2012)

Someone posted this, without attribution, on Facebook, and I thought it was the saddest poem I'd ever read. A woman is walking in a field where deer graze; it could be any American poem of the last forty years. Then:

> And never in the river the same water over a rock.
> To be lonely like your own hand. To be so
> goddamn lonely with just a little information.

Everything flows. I have read this poem dozens of times, and its author has become a close friend, but the final lines retain a mystery I don't ever want to find my way out of:

> At certain times of day a field can blind you.
> So I walked, uncharacteristically slow.
> You couldn't know how slow I walked.

Alphaville
"Forever Young" (1984)

Like "1999" and "99 Luftballons," a soundtrack for growing up caught between two different sick lies about freedom.

Yehuda Amichai
"A Letter" (1976)

For this verse, on its own as desolate and true as any poem ever written:

> To live is to build a ship and a harbor
> at the same time. And to finish the harbor
> long after the ship has gone down.

Anonymous
"In those days, in those far-off days" (c. 1800 BCE)

A poem about Bilgames, the Sumerian name for Gilgamesh, in which even life after death is characterized by the repetition that structures the verses:

> after he had set sail, after he had set sail,
> after the father had set sail for the Netherworld,
> after the god Enki had set sail for the Netherworld,
> on the lord the small ones poured down,
> on Enki the big ones poured down—

The warrior Bilgames has defeated some evil spirits that lived in a blown-down willow tree the goddess Inanna found on the bank of the Euphrates after a storm ("a solitary tree, a solitary willow, a solitary tree"). With the wood he fashions two toys—scholars don't agree on what kind—and plays with them all day until the girls bringing him water complain to the gods, who cause the toys to fall through a hole into the Netherworld, as toys will. Bilgames weeps over their loss until his servant Enkidu volunteers to go and fetch them, a prototype of Odysseus, Orpheus, Dante pilgrim. At the end of the poem he reports what he has seen to his master: " 'If I am to [tell] you the way things are ordered in the Netherworld, / O sit you down and weep!' 'Then let me sit down and weep!' " The final lines pronounce the fate of souls who die by fire: " 'Did you see the man who was burnt to death?' 'I did not see him. . . . / His ghost was not there, his smoke went up to the heavens.' " And the poem seems to blow through the millennia to Paul Celan's "Death Fugue," in which those who died in the ovens dig a grave in the clouds.

Anonymous
[Westron wynde when wylle thow blow] (c. 16th century?)

> Westron wynde when wylle thow blow
> the smalle rayne downe can Rayne
> Cryst yf my love were in my Armys
> And I yn my bed A gayne

Along with its fellow Norton Anthology mainstay "Nou goth sonne under wode," this poem was my introduction to the medieval lyric. It first shows up in an early sixteenth-century manuscript, set to music, but it feels older to me. I could note the windy alliteration and assonance of the first line, the rain-like repetition of the second, with its driving iambs. That's all fine, but it's the sort of junk that kills poetry for undergraduates. I love the poem because it is a perfect condensation of loneliness—a kind of pop song.

Matsuo Bashō
["Even in Kyoto"] (c. 1689)

> Even in Kyoto—
> hearing the cuckoo's cry—
> I long for Kyoto

Bashō nails in three lines an emotional complex for which Wordsworth needed one hundred sixty. (Everyone should read Makoto Ueda's magnificent *Bashō and His Interpreters*—did you know the Japanese hold moon-viewing parties?)

Beastie Boys
"(You Gotta) Fight for Your Right (to Party!)" (1986)

This song hit my junior high with the force of a bomb, leaving the entire student body divided—for or against. A novelty song with the gusto of "Yakety Yak," which is to say: novel, but not (only) a joke.

Beyoncé
Beyoncé (2013) and "Formation" (2016)

If the most vital artist of a given historical period is the one who most tantalizingly embodies that period's contradictions, look no further than a zillionaire who cops Black Lives Matter brio and Panthers optics while appearing to stand for nothing so much as the spectacle of money ("The spectacle is money *for contemplation only*"—Guy Debord). The music, though—beats that skitter like the insects Hollywood thinks aliens look like then drop booms that shudder city blocks—the music has its own ideas.

Big Black
Songs About Fucking (1987)

I don't trust moralists who can't hear Britney Spears over the roar of their prejudices, but this record is the guitar equivalent of the final shoot-out in *The Wild Bunch*.

Elizabeth Bishop
The Complete Poems: 1927–1979 (1983)

It's hard to get a handle on Elizabeth Bishop, because she will remove the handle and stick it in a poem, and soon she's telling you what tree the wood comes from, and what she saw on the road to the village where the woodcutter lives, and what objects were lying about in his yard, and who was playing with them, and what the town where they were manufactured is most famous for, and how it got its name. Watching closely, looking and looking her "infant sight away."

Gwendolyn Brooks
"The Blackstone Rangers" (1968)

Brooks first presents the Chicago street gang "As Seen by Disciplines," or by those whose concern is order, categories. To cops and sociologists, the Rangers are simply "[s]ores in the city / that do not want to heal." This image is countered in the following section, as the gangsters "construct, strangely, a monstrous pearl or grace" in the "translations of the night." But it's the "Gang Girls" of the third section who bring Brooks to a boil as she urges them to give up their delusions of glamour:

> Settle for sandwiches! settle for stocking caps!
> for sudden blood, aborted carnival,
> the props and niceties of non-loneliness—
> the rhymes of Leaning.

Like Stevens and Frank O'Hara, Brooks inherits "Leaning" from Whitman. Here it rhymes with "gleaning"—gathering and valuing the discarded, overlooked bits. Those whom America leaves behind lean on, prop up, rhyme with, shoulder to shoulder, one another.

Peter Brötzmann Octet
Machine Gun (1968)

In college, this and the first Clash record were my I Hate Everything music. No one I've played the opening blast for can believe they're hearing saxophones.

Anne Carson
"Irony Is Not Enough: Essay on My Life as Catherine Deneuve (2nd draft)" (2000)

The speaker is in love with a girl, a student in her seminar. Life is a movie, or at least something staged, outside her, her role played by Catherine Deneuve. The girl is a mess, crazy with missing her boyfriend in Paris. Deneuve asks about him, and the exchange captures desire's particularities with the concision of a Pet Shop Boys lyric:

> *What do you want?*

> *Want to be in the same room with him.*

> *I admire your clarity.*

> *Gottago.*

Shaun Cassidy
Shaun Cassidy (1977)

The first record I ever owned. I was obsessed with "Da Doo Ron Ron" (I didn't know it was a cover, hadn't heard of Phil Spector), so my mom took me to a record store. Wichita, the summer of *Star Wars*. Is it possible I stood in that light, beneath an Ace Frehley poster, among Kansans with major hair, such unlikely cars coursing past outside? Chelsey Minnis: "When I die a bunch of images from the '70s will pass before my eyes."

Ray Charles
Modern Sounds in Country and Western Music (1962)

Together with Aretha Franklin's *I Never Loved a Man the Way I Love You* and an Otis Redding compilation, this record flipped my teenage script. Between Charles's "Well, you know if I could *mmmm-mm-mmm-hmmm-hmm* like a mourning dove" and Aretha's stratospheric free flights into the wordless on "Baby, Baby, Baby," it was months before I listened to Hüsker Dü again.

Lucille Clifton
"[surely i am able to write poems]" (2004)

> whenever i begin
> "the trees wave their knotted branches
> and . . ." why
> is there under that poem always
> an other poem?

"By emphatically separating themselves from the empirical world, their other," Adorno wrote, artworks "bear witness that that world itself should be other than it is; they are the unconscious schemata of that world's transformation."

Samuel Taylor Coleridge
"Frost at Midnight" (1798)

"For if words are not THINGS, they are LIVING POWERS," Coleridge wrote. The final lines of his greatest poem are proof of life:

> whether the eave-drops fall
> Heard only in the trances of the blast,
> Or if the secret ministry of frost
> Shall hang them up in silent icicles,
> Quietly shining to the quiet Moon.

John Coltrane and Johnny Hartman
John Coltrane and Johnny Hartman (1963)

The dreamiest, creamiest sounds ever made by the mouths of men.

Miles Davis
The Complete Live at the Plugged Nickel 1965 (1995)

My favorite Miles records—*Milestones*, *Jack Johnson*, *Get Up with It*—astound and disconcert, but they're not hard to understand. This music, though—seven hours from a two-night gig in dead-winter Chicago, with Wayne Shorter and Tony Williams playing like gods—I've been trying to figure out for two decades. It helped when I stopped thinking of it as "jazz."

Death
The Sound of Perseverance (1998)

In the state with the prettiest name, the late Chuck Schuldiner (who found Satanism silly and loved animals) basically invented death metal. My favorite metal record after Slayer's *Reign in Blood*—proggy, sinister, with on-a-dime swaps: rocket-to-Siberia melodies for minor-key riffs for smokestack brutalism.

Lana Del Rey
Honeymoon (2015)

The camera discovers Gene Tierney floating facedown in a swimming pool, her white dress billowing in waves of light and shadow. It pans up and through a window into a dim ballroom, tracks slowly toward the stage, on which a young woman stands swaying beneath a spotlight. Her white dress sparkles like champagne. She's singing a song—hesitant, languorous—not to the sparse audience, but to someone inside her: "And we could cruise / To the news / Pico Boulevard / In your used / Little bullet car / If we choose." A few men at the table nearest the stage look at one another with arched eyebrows: "Is this broad for real?" She is, she isn't—it's a distinction for fools. The camera slides away from her, back out to the shimmering pool, now empty. Did someone remove the corpse? *Was* it a corpse? The camera lifts, revealing the broad galaxy of Los Angeles glitzy beneath the Hollywood sign. The singer's voice, fainter now, drifts off into the night.

Diane di Prima
Revolutionary Letters (1971)

How I learned to stop worrying and love poems about "molotov cocktails, flamethrowers, bombs."

Dan Fogelberg
"Leader of the Band" (1981)

This is not a good song. This is the worst song, a sodden tribute to Fogelberg's father. But one February night in 1983, we lost power to our modest A-frame house near Woodland Park, Colorado. It was twenty below outside, and we kids slept huddled in front of the fireplace. My dad, a little drunk, put a song on my battery-powered boom box and told me to pay attention to the lyrics. The lyrics are gunk: "a thund'ring, velvet hand," "his gentle means of sculpting souls." But I didn't hear that then; I heard what my dad heard in it—love and loss, fathers and sons.

Franco & le TPOK Jazz
Francophonic, Vol. 1: 1953–1980 (2008) and *Vol. 2: 1980–1989* (2009)

The DNA helix of intertwined electric guitars—Skynyrd, Crazy Horse, Funkadelic, Derek and the Dominos, Drive-By Truckers—is my favorite sound. So on the several comps I own featuring the Congolese colossus Franco Luambo Makiadi and his soukous band, originally named OK Jazz, I listen for the *sebene*, an instrumental bridge on which guitarists repeat hypnotic hooks or improvise. "On entre OK, on sort KO," as an early song title has it. It's barely a metaphor.

Future
DS2 (2015)

More proof that "avant-garde" has become a meaningless descriptor. This alienated industrial clatter shot to number one on the *Billboard* 200 chart. Future's clouded mutter matches the medicinal desolation of his lyrics: "I know the devil is real, I know the devil is real / I take a dose of them pills and I get real low in the field."

Gilberto Gil and Jorge Ben
Gil e Jorge (1975)

I love *Tusk, Exile on Main St, There's a Riot Goin' On, Innervisions, Pink Flag, Best of Dolly Parton, Jack Johnson, Led Zeppelin IV, Fun House, Master of Reality, Tonight's the Night, Superfly, Darkness on the Edge of Town, One Nation Under a Groove, Pretzel Logic, Another Green World, Dixie Chicken*, a hundred disco and punk records. But this undomesticated jam session is, I insist, the best pop record of the '70s.

Jean-Luc Godard
Le Mépris (Contempt) (1963)

Jack Palance, playing an American film producer, hires Fritz Lang, playing himself, to direct an adaptation of *The Odyssey*. "I like gods," Palance says as they watch a rough cut. "I like them very much." He's talking to one. Another is behind the camera. A bust of Homer flashes on the screen.

Al Green
The Belle Album (1977)

In college, we played the equally mighty *Call Me* on an ill-conceived nightlong drive through Wyoming until my friend's Dodge Dart's tape deck vomited it in ribbons. I return more often now to this airy record with its beat made out of light. "The academic study of prayer may lead a man to pray," H. A. Williams said. Listening to these songs may lead a person to believe in grace.

Guns N' Roses
Appetite for Destruction (1987)

Some of my friends were too cool for this band, but the first time I heard "Sweet Child o' Mine" on MTV, I would've traded all my Ramones records to hear it again.

Donald Hall
"Weeds and Peonies" (1998)

Hall's poems are well-behaved meditations on love and snow and loss and barns. I hate them. This one concludes a series of elegies for Hall's wife, the poet Jane Kenyon, dead of leukemia at forty-seven. The peonies she planted have bloomed after her death, an irony too cruel to resist. The final lines find an objective correlative whose metaphorical and syntactical precision blasts my aesthetic objections away:

> I pace beside weeds
> and snowy peonies, staring at Mount Kearsarge
> where you climbed wearing purple hiking boots.
> "Hurry back. Be careful, climbing down."
> Your peonies lean their vast heads westward
> as if they might topple. Some topple.

Jimi Hendrix
"Hey Baby (New Rising Sun)" (1971)

If the extraterrestrials have their priorities straight, when they get here the first thing they'll want to know is what rock and roll is. I'll play them this.

Hole
Live Through This (1994)

It's twenty years ago and I'm looking across Zapotec ruins. On my Walkman, Courtney Love snarls and shrieks and finally whispers:

> And some day you will ache like I ache / And some day you will ache like I ache / And some day you will ache like I ache / AND SOME DAY YOU WILL ACHE LIKE I ACHE / AND SOME DAY YOU WILL ACHE LIKE I ACHE / AND SOME DAY YOU WILL ACHE LIKE I ACHE / AND SOME DAY YOU WILL ACHE LIKE I ACHE / Some day you will ache like I ache.

Gerard Manley Hopkins
"Spring and Fall" (1880)

Dedicated "to a young child," Margaret, who is "gríeving / Over Goldengrove unleaving." It's a bit false ("not founded on any real incident," you don't say; has any child ever wept over fallen leaves?) and a bit sententious (all sorrow *springs* from man's *Fall* into original sin). But the poem, my introduction to literature's favorite Jesuit priest, is a high-tension-wire act—a rhythmic-syllabic riot of measured, melancholy calm:

Nor mouth had, no nor mind, expressed
What heart heard of, ghost guessed:
It ís the blight man was born for,
It is Margaret you mourn for.

Skip James
"Devil Got My Woman" (1931)

Sometimes I think this song defines the limits of what is humanly possible. Sometimes I think it exceeds them.

Kix
"Don't Close Your Eyes" (1988)

The hair-metal power ballad was one of the few art forms of the late twentieth century to flirt successfully with transcendence. Hear also Def Leppard's "Love Bites," Cinderella's "Don't Know What You Got (Till It's Gone)" and "Coming Home," and, of course, Poison's "Every Rose Has Its Thorn."

August Kleinzahler
"Sleeping It Off in Rapid City" (2008)

This poem is a hundred-car pile-up on a frozen interstate in a blizzard. It begins "On a 700 foot thick shelf of Cretaceous pink sandstone" and ends six pages later in "[t]he dead solid center of the universe / At the heart of the heart of America." It's "God Bless America" as Ginsberg's "bop kabbalah," the cosmos instinctively vibrating at Kleinzahler's feet outside a "closed dinosaur shop" in South Dakota, where a Triceratops tape-loop roars through the night, where Kevin Costner cries *"Tatanka, Tatanka,"* where "[t]he Lambs of Christ are among us / You can tell by the billboards / The billboards with fetuses, out there on the highway," where semis haul "toothpaste, wheels of Muenster, rapeseed oil . . . across the Cretaceous hogback" past "[t]he ghosts of 98 foot long Titans and Minutemen." Bless the commerce, Kleinzahler says, bless Nixon and Mao and Crazy Horse, for this is "sanctified ground" and "We're right on top of it, baby."

David Markson
Wittgenstein's Mistress (1988)

Kate is, or believes herself to be, the last animal on earth. And yet she spends much of her time traveling to the great art museums: "There is one painting at the Prado by Rogier van der Weyden, *The Descent from the Cross*, that I had wished to see again." It's the recurrence of a certain tag that most moves me: "Through another window at its opposite side the rosy-fingered dawn awakens me"; "The next morning, when dawn appeared, I was quite content to consider it a rosy-fingered dawn." This idea harrows me: even if you were as alone as it is possible to get, art might continue to function as equipment for living. Is that true? What is art without other people? The Homeric signal pulsing from three thousand years ago finding one last grateful receiver continues to broadcast long after she is gone, *ars longa, occasio praeceps*, blinking, blinking into heat death and who knows.

Mastodon
Remission (2002)

Riffage. Huge, mud-caked barn doors of riffage. Aluminum siding of riffage slicing through trees of riffage in a hurricane of riffage. The American mastodon (the name means "nipple tooth," which would also be a good name for a metal band) weighed around five tons, which is exactly how much the Atlanta band's debut record weighs. But there's a progressive complexity here too—Bill Kelliher (guitars) and Brann Dailor (drums) trample forests then carefully diagram each leaf.

Curtis Mayfield
"Move On Up" (1970)

July 28, 2016: retired marine general John Allen addresses the Democratic Convention at the Wells Fargo Center in Philadelphia. His bellicose speech is a paean to the American military—"the shining example of America at our very best"—and its "weapons and equipment." When he finishes speaking, the auditorium fills with music. You think: They can't really be playing *this* after *that*. But they are. On a popular social media platform, writer Elliott Sharp summed up the venality of the moment, of these people: "They played a Curtis Mayfield song after that fascist DNC war speech because nothing matters to them."

Mother McCollum
"Jesus Is My Air-o-plane" (1930)

McCollum's slide guitar plunks two pebbles into a pond and she's off riding ripples. No donkey this time around—the savior's "coming through in an air-o-plane," gliding downward to brightness on Easter wings.

Chelsey Minnis
"[Five Poems]," *Coconut Magazine* #12 (2008)

I'm a fan of Minnis's *Poemland*, in which a few of these pieces appear, and which says things like "If you want to be a poem-writer then I don't know why." But the line of hers I want on my headstone didn't make the cut: "Some lives are too hard to be lived without cigarettes."

The National
"Don't Swallow the Cap" (2013)

I know: no range, no risk, no *rock*. "Sad white man music," a friend calls it. Matt Berninger's clever lines are so calculated someone should give him an MFA. But I'm a sucker for the kicker: "And if you want / To see me cry / Play *Let It Be* / Or *Nevermind*."

New York Dolls
New York Dolls (1973) and *Too Much Too Soon* (1974)

Let the Dolls stand for all the bands that stood for freedom when I was seventeen—Television, the Clash, the Raincoats, the Ramones, LiLiPUT, the Pretenders, Gang of Four, the Mekons, the Jam, Elvis Costello & the Attractions, X, Wire, the Stooges, the Adverts, a dozen more—any of whom, despite their differences, could have said, with the Dolls' David Johansen, that wanting too many things is what makes you human.

Michael Palmer
Sun (1988)

The good news that Palmer's work (and, in a more drastic but related fashion, Susan Howe's) delivered to me as a young poet manqué had little to do with "the materiality of the signifier." It was rather the joy of words gone wild, free to roam whence they would—"F for alphabet, Z for A, an H in an arbor"—but trailing always the ghosts of rhetoric and emotion: "Say this. I was born on an island among the dead. I learned language on this island but did not speak on this island. I am writing to you from this island."

Pet Shop Boys
Very (1993)

The after-party. Or the wake.

Tom Pickard
"Hawthorn" (2007)

It opens like a ballad Francis Child missed or Fairport Convention forgot to record:

> there is a hawthorn on a hill
> there is a hawthorn growing
> it set its roots against the wind
> the worrying wind that's blowing
> its berries are red its blossom so white
> I thought that it was snowing

The rest of the poem never quite catches up to that. How could it?

Vasko Popa
"Horse" (1952)

A poem about a horse can begin "Usually / He has eight legs"—? That was all I needed to know; nothing was ever the same.

Ezra Pound
Cathay (1915)

The magic of Pound's not-quite translations from the Chinese (and one from the Anglo-Saxon) renders their Casaubon-vexing inaccuracies insignificant. I hear the unacknowledged Whitman ("least of all Walt Whitman," Eliot wrote of Pound's influences) behind lines like these:

> And I, wrapped in brocade, went to sleep with my head on
>   his lap,
> And my spirit so high it was all over the heavens,
> And before the end of the day we were scattered like stars,
>   or rain.

That's from "Exile's Letter," which taught me how beauty is related to syntax:

> And if you ask how I regret that parting:
> It is like the flowers falling at Spring's end
> Confused, whirled in a tangle.
> What is the use of talking, and there is no end of talking,
> There is no end of things in the heart.

A "proper" translation of these lines might get us closer to Li Bai's original, but the letter killeth and the spirit giveth life.

Ezra Pound
Translation of "Praise Song of the Buck Hare," anonymous Siberian folksong (1938)

The origins of this folksong are impossible to trace. Pound found the poem in a German translation of a Russian translation of an oral original sung among the Teleut people of Siberia. A monster riff of self-inflation, it zooms to life and never hits the brakes:

> I am the buck-hare, I am,
> The shore is my playground.
> Green underwood is my feeding.
>
> I am the buck-hare, I am,
> What's that damn man got wrong with him?
> Skin with no hair on, that's his trouble.

Pound makes the hare sound like a jackrabbit disparaging cowboys: "What's that fool got the matter with him? / Can't find the road! Ain't got no road he CAN find." Then he sounds like John Berryman's Henry rewriting Stevens's "Bantams in Pine-Woods": "I am the buck-hare, I am, / I got my wood-road, / I got my form."

Prince (1958–2016)

> The rain in Minneapolis is rain-
> colored. The poor, purple in the cold,
> are lifted up by no white bird.
> Ghostface recites the cancer rates
> while Prince commands the tide to turn—
> our paisley priest, our Swinburne.

That's the last stanza of my poem "New Bridge Strategies." I know it's bad form to quote myself at such length, but it serves a purpose. I allude in these lines to James Wright's "Minneapolis Poem" and to the twelfth-century anecdote of King Canute's demonstration of God's supreme power (he orders the sea to turn back, knowing his secular power holds no sway). The vanity of human wishes was one of Prince's great themes, often the one on which hinged his dominant theme of carnality.

This was missing from many elegies and eulogies, especially those written to order in the hours after his death. Not, of course, that Prince ever lost all his mirth. But many of his biggest hits vibe all-is-vanity melancholy. It's there in "1999" ("Everybody's got a bomb / We could all die any day"—might as well dance our lives away); "Purple Rain" ("I never meant 2 cause u any sorrow / I never meant 2 cause u any pain"—unspoken corollary: but I did); "Gotta Broken Heart Again" ("Once your love has gone away / There ain't nothing, nothing left to say"); "Little Red Corvette" ("I guess I should've known / By the way u parked your car sideways / That it wouldn't last"—the pure poetry of details).

And it's all over "Sometimes It Snows in April," a blown field miles outside pop's recognized borders. It's theater—an elegy for Christopher Tracy, the character played by Prince in his insane film *Under the Cherry Moon*—and all the more effective for it. Who knows who the singer is supposed to be? Who cares? Listen to the way he sings: "I used 2 cry 4 Tracy because I want to see

him again / But sometimes sometimes life ain't always the way."
The grief in his voice on these stone-simple lines is not fictional—if
anything it's too real, like the way he screams "Do you want him!
Or do you want me! Cuz I want you!" on "The Beautiful Ones."
Prince pushed himself into the red at moments like these, became
something larger than the radio could contain, an earth wire, an
overload.

Most of all it's there in his guitar, an instrument he made cry
like no one else since Hendrix. His solos are where everything in
his music zeroes in on totality—parties weren't meant to last, you're
on your own, something doesn't compute, you done me wrong, we
wouldn't be satisfied, love will always leave you lonely; but also I
want you, the rain sounds so cool when it hits the barn roof, I'm
gonna listen to my body tonight, I'll die in your arms. A rip cord
elegance on "Purple Rain," the physical graffiti that kick off "When
Doves Cry," a demolition of "Honky Tonk Women" on YouTube,
an end-times power drive on *Emancipation*'s overlooked cover of
"One of Us."

If a guitar solo can be a poem—but no. Prince wasn't Milton to
Jimi's or Sly Stone's Shakespeare. He transcended analogy: he was
Prince. Our paisley priest has punched a higher floor.

Public Enemy
It Takes a Nation of Millions to Hold Us Back (1988)

The first rap album I owned; purchased on used cassette for two
dollars at Colorado Springs' Independent Annex. I put it in my tape
deck and giggled at the corny Brit trying to fire a crowd: "Let me
hear you make some noise!" Then the aptly named production team
the Bomb Squad dropped an arsenal on my speakers and I stopped
giggling.

Thomas Rhett
"Learned It from the Radio" (2015)

Shit jobs, cheating lovers, heavy drinking, rolling in the hay, rolling the windows down and singing along with the radio on a Friday night—the standard repertoire gets a downright Bon Jovial spin from the guitar bonanza that is twenty-first-century country radio. Miranda Lambert, Eric Church, Keith Urban, Brad Paisley, Maren Morris, Jason Aldean, Toby Keith, and a dozen more sing in the teeth of the dark times. And they sing about the songs and what they learned from them, as in Thomas Rhett's paean to 4-wheel drive, the DJs in "little static towns," and "the speakers in the door."

Rihanna
Anti (2016)

We'll be parsing the vocals on this album for years—the dropped consonants, the lines thrown like daggers. On "Higher," Rihanna sings with an abandon you never hear on the radio anymore, as if she hadn't known she was being recorded, or didn't care. My friend Jen Vafidis writes: "I'd say I identify with her, I often have 'a little bit too much to say,' but how can anyone truly identify with Rihanna? Why would anyone want to? You wish you didn't feel the things she's singing about. This is why she is my favorite performer these days. She makes me sad, happy, ashamed, and willing all at once."

The Rolling Stones
Exile on Main St (1972)

The Stones were my Beatles; I couldn't begin to say which album mattered most. This is the one that kept me company through six

European countries the summer I was twenty-two, sleeping on train platforms and cathedral steps with my Walkman stuffed down the front of my pants so I'd wake up if anyone tried to steal it.

The Ronettes
"Be My Baby" (1963)

Forget the post-Beatles '60s and the '70s—the years 1954 to 1965 were rock and roll's greatest decade ("rock and roll" as shorthand for the wild flowering fusion of R&B, doo-wop, gospel, rockabilly, the kitchen sink). The "5" Royales, the Coasters, the Drifters, Elvis, Ray Charles, James Brown, the Shirelles, the Beach Boys, the Chantels, Elmore James, Martha and the Vandellas, the Miracles, Darlene Love, a hundred more. From drummer Hal Blaine's opening enfilade, everything about "Be My Baby" is shell-shocked: a sound caught between big dreams and last chances, on the short list of perfect rock songs with "That's All Right," "Down in Mexico," "Say It," "People Get Ready," "I Think We're Alone Now," "Wouldn't It Be Nice," "Gimme Shelter," "Thunder Road," "Love to Love You Baby," "Surrender," "Billie Jean," "Jump," and "Swallowed by the Cracks."

Mary Ruefle
Selected Poems (2011)

Ruefle makes art where the obvious—"I was born in a hospital. I stank"—meets the ineffable—"My inability to express myself / is astounding." Opposite banks of a single river, the poem a Tarzan-whoop vine-veering between them. Of the lunar crater Tycho she says, "I have never been there." Of our residence on Earth: "I was going to ardently pursue this day / but you know how these things go."

Moacir Santos
Coisas (1965)

The great lost jazz album of the '60s—*The Penguin Guide to Jazz* has no entry for Santos; *Coisas* wasn't issued on CD until 2004 and promptly went out of print. Santos grew up an orphan in rural poverty in Brazil and became a composer whose arranging genius rivaled that of Ellington. You can hear samba and bossa nova and Rio jazz, and some of the melody lines remind me of Mingus, but this record is deeply its own thing, like the crocodile Mark Antony describes for Lepidus.

James Schuyler
Collected Poems (1995)

My favorite poet these last several years, Schuyler knew that wishing for too many things is what makes you human: "I wish it was 1938 or '39 again / and Bernie was sleeping / With me in the tent at the back of the yard"; "I wish / I could send you a bundle of orange lilies / to paint"; "I wish one could press / snowflakes in a book like flowers." He constantly takes himself by surprise, revising himself by reevaluating his desires: "I wish I could take an engine apart and reassemble it. / I also wish I sincerely wanted to. I don't."

Simple Minds
"See the Lights" (1991)

For some reason, this generic anthem was all I listened to one miserable summer.

Frank Sinatra
Songs for Young Lovers (1954)

And *Swing Easy!* and *Songs for Swingin' Lovers!* and *A Swingin' Affair!* and *Only the Lonely* and *Come Fly with Me* and *Come Dance with Me!* and *Sinatra at the Sands*—the catalog is as rich as the voice. This one has "My Funny Valentine," two-and-a-half minutes of genius phrasing and articulation. Dig how many moods he swings through as the final "stay" shades into "each day is Valentine's Day."

Sister Sledge
"Lost in Music" (1979)

Disco was punker than punk, dance music spun oppositional courtesy of good old American bigotry (cf. Machine's transcendent "There but for the Grace of God Go I"). Never mind the Sex Pistols—I'll take Sylvester, Vicki Sue Robinson, Andrea True, Donna Summer, Diana Ross, Anita Ward, and, most of all, Nile Rodgers and Bernard Edwards. Especially lost in lyric sway with four sisters from Philly who invite you to shove your job and join a band.

Bruce Springsteen & the E Street Band
"Lost in the Flood" (1975)

The live version on *Hammersmith Odeon, London '75*. A singer—a punk, a grease monkey—slams a spike called the E Street Band directly into his bloodstream, where it surfs the sounds of his nervous system. The resulting animal is tight as the Famous Flames. Its voice is a thin tendril at first, but it snakes into the music's chinks and hollows until it chokes the sun: "Hey kid you think that's oil?" it screams. "Maaaaan that ain't oil that's blood."

Wallace Stevens
"The Man with the Blue Guitar," Canto XXV (1937)

A rumpus, a rollick, a roll in the hay:

> They did not know the grass went round.
> The cats had cats and the grass turned gray
>
> And the world had worlds, ai, this-a-way:
> The grass turned green and the grass turned gray.
>
> And the nose is eternal, that-a-way.
> Things as they were, things as they are,
>
> Things as they will be by and by . . .
> A fat thumb beats out ai-yi-yi.

Superchunk
"Me & You & Jackie Mittoo" (2013)

"I hate music, what is it worth / Can't bring anyone back to this earth," Mac McCaughan bellows as the drums kick in, and his grief is a brick wall. Then a wrecking ball: "But I got nothing else, so I guess here we go." And the song opens into the past, the singer and his friends crammed into the back of a van, back when a half hour in the Record Exchange was world enough and time. It ends abruptly, barely two minutes in, with McCaughan repeating the first two lines, revising them slightly—"It can't bring you back to this earth"—and all you can think to do is play the song again and hope it comes out different this time.

Jonathan Swift
"Mary the Cook-Maid's Letter to Dr. Sheridan" (1723)

See also "To Their Excellencies The Lords Justices of Ireland: The Humble Petition of Frances Harris, Who Must Starve, and Die a Maid If It Miscarries"—exquisite examples of doggerel done doggone good.

Ulver
Bergtatt (1995)

Black metal people who don't like people who like black metal can like.

Henry Vaughan
"The Night" (1650)

The final stanza, Jonathan F. S. Post says, shows Vaughan's "reluctance to dissolve into rapture"; for Geoffrey Hill, it's "the envisioning of perplexity itself":

> There is in God (some say)
> A deep, but dazzling darkness; As men here
> Say it is late and dusky, because they
> See not all clear.
> O for that Night! Where I in him
> Might live invisible and dim!

The parenthetical is both humble and guarded, resistant to certainty as well as to easy rapture. *We*, of course, are too wise to contort ourselves into perplexities concerning God, whose content we know to be exhausted by what "men here say." Our instruments have vanquished the night; we see perfectly clearly.

Wham!
"Freedom" (1984)

Forget the '60s and '70s—the '80s were rock and roll's greatest decade. Prince, Madonna, Jackson, Springsteen, but also ABC, Pet Shop Boys, Kix, Eric B. and Rakim, New Order, Iron Maiden, Don Henley, Public Enemy, DeBarge, John Waite, Grandmaster Flash, Tina Turner, Van Halen, the Beastie Boys, Slayer, and a hundred more. And somehow the son of a Cypriot restaurateur from London made the best Motown record Motown never made.

John Wilmot, Earl of Rochester
"The Imperfect Enjoyment" (c. 1672)

English Renaissance poetry received impotence verse from Ovid via Christopher Marlowe ("like one dead it lay, / Drouping more then a Rose puld yesterday"). The genre enjoyed a vogue in the late seventeenth century; see also Aphra Behn's "The Disappointment," originally misattributed to Rochester ("In vain he Toils, in vain Commands, / Th' Insensible fell weeping in his Hands"). Before Rochester's rose can droop, it blooms too early:

> In liquid raptures I dissolve all o'er,
> Melt into sperm, and spend at every pore.
> A touch from any part of her had done 't:
> Her hand, her foot, her very look's a cunt.

His lover, named Corinna after Ovid's, gently chides him "and from her body wipes the clammy joys." His shame prevents him from rising again to the occasion:

> Eager desires confound my first intent,
> Succeeding shame does more success prevent,
> And rage at last confirms me impotent.

In a proto-Freudian paradox, desire gets in the way of intention. Freud saw impotence as the result of conflict between love and sexual desire. The "sensual current" must debase its object in order to find expression. As Rochester recalls past conquests, he turns his misogyny on himself, railing against his recalcitrant prick, wishing on it venereal ulcers and the dreaded stone. He ends with the hope that Corinna might be paid the "debt to pleasure" she is owed:

> May'st thou ne'er piss, who did refuse to spend
> When all my joys did on false thee depend.
>   And may ten thousand abler pricks agree
> To do the wronged Corinna right for thee.

Neil Young and Crazy Horse
"Cowgirl in the Sand" (1969)

In the late '70s, in a house in the woods, my dad would blast this song to holy hell, shaking the pines outside. I remember him sitting there, a can of Coors Light in one hand, nodding along, glazed with nirvana. Still in his twenties, Christ, he couldn't have known a goddamned thing. But he could hear this for what it is—a war, a summa, the alpha and omega of rock and roll. The phonograph needle, the damage done.

ACKNOWLEDGMENTS

This book wouldn't exist without Virginia Heffernan and Ben Loehnen. Popovers on me.

Zach Baron, Garnette Cadogan, Oren Izenberg, Anthony Madrid, Anahid Nersessian, Ben Ratliff, and Jen Vafidis provided rich and thoughtful comments on drafts of some of these pieces. They're crazy smart and I'm lucky as hell to know them. I'm also indebted to Paige Ackerson-Kiely, Jennifer Days, Mark Fletcher, William Junker, Julia Kardon, Laura Kolb, Joshua Kotin, Christa Robbins, and John Wilson. And to Katherine, so important.

Thanks to the editors of the following journals, in which some of these essays and reviews, or parts of them, first appeared, often in different form: *Bookforum*, *Harper's Magazine*, *London Review of Books*, *Modern Philology*, *The New York Observer*, *Poetry*, *Post Road*, *Spin*.

"Hooked Up," "How to Write a Charles Simic Poem," "No Taste of My Own," a brief section of "Equipment for Sinking," and the Prince entry in "Playlist," originally appeared, in whole or part, under different titles, in *Chicago Tribune Printers Row*.

NOTES

1 Annie Dillard, *Holy the Firm* (New York: Harper, 1977), 50.

2 Harold Bloom, *Agon* (Oxford: Galaxy Books, 1982), 19.

3 Kenneth Burke, *The Philosophy of Literary Form* (Berkeley: Univ. of California Press, 1974), 61.

4 Burke, 298.

5 Boethius, *The Consolation of Philosophy*, trans. P. G. Walsh (Oxford: Oxford University Press, 2008), xix.

6 Adam Phillips, *Missing Out: In Praise of the Unlived Life* (New York: Picador, 2013), 130.

7 Burke, 61.

8 Roland Greene et al., eds., *The Princeton Encyclopedia of Poetry and Poetics*, 4th ed. (Princeton, NJ: Princeton University Press, 2012), 497.

9 Quoted in Angela Leighton, *On Form* (New York: Oxford University Press, 2007), 24. If you're interested in the history of the concept of form and its maddening elusiveness, you need to check out this book.

10 Burke, 44.

11 Geoffrey Hill, *Collected Critical Writings* (New York: Oxford University Press, 2009), 497.

12 Adam Phillips, *Promises, Promises: Essays on Psychoanalysis and Literature* (New York: Basic Books, 2001), 31.

13 Leo Bersani and Adam Phillips, *Intimacies* (Chicago: University of Chicago Press, 2008), 117.

14 John Jeremiah Sullivan, "The Ballad of Geeshie and Elvie," *New York Times Magazine*, April 13, 2014.

15 Eisenberg, 53–54.

16 Friedrich Kittler, *Gramophone, Film, Typewriter* (Stanford: Stanford University Press, 1999), 29.

17 I have relied throughout this section on Lisa Gitelman, *Scripts, Grooves, and Writing Machines: Representing Technology in the Edison Era* (Stanford: Stanford University Press, 1999), and Michael North, *Camera Works: Photography and the Twentieth-Century Word* (New York: Oxford University Press, 2005).

18 Elijah Wald, *Escaping the Delta: Robert Johnson and the Invention of the Blues* (New York: Amistad, 2004), xxxi.

19 Ibid., 171.

20 Greil Marcus, *Mystery Train: Images of America in Rock 'n' Roll Music*, 6th ed. (New York: Plume, 2015), 31.

21 Ibid.

22 Dom Gregory Dix, *The Shape of the Liturgy*, 2nd revised ed. (London: Bloomsbury, 2005), 599.

23 John Jeremiah Sullivan, *Pulphead* (New York: Farrar, Straus and Giroux, 2011), 122.

24 See http://thequietus.com/articles/07073-wolves-in-the-throne-room-interview?fb_comment_id=10150391339698799_23961114#ffa58a4c1522a6.

25 Erik Davis, "Deep Eco-Metal," *Slate* (November 13, 2007), http://www.slate.com/articles/arts/music_box/2007/11/deep_ecometal.html.

26 See http://www.tarpaulinsky.com/Summer05/Spahr/Juliana_Spahr.html.

27 Chuck Eddy, *Stairway to Hell* (Boston: Da Capo Press), 1.

28 Greil Marcus, *Stranded: Rock and Roll for a Desert Island* (Boston: Da Capo Press), 277.

29 See http://www.publishersweekly.com/978-0-374-23531-4.

30 Ellen Willis, *Out of the Vinyl Deeps* (Minneapolis: University of Minnesota Press), 115.

31 *Princeton Encyclopedia*, 1182, 1191.

32 Hugh Kenner, "Rhyme: An Unfinished Monograph," *Common Knowledge* 10, no. 3, (Fall 2004): 378.

33 Ernest Fenollosa and Ezra Pound, *The Chinese Written Character as a Medium for Poetry: A Critical Edition*, eds. Haun Saussy, Jonathan Stalling, and Lucas Klein (New York: Fordham University Press, 2008), 138.

34 Gillian White, *Lyric Shame: The "Lyric" Subject of Contemporary American Poetry* (Cambridge, MA: Harvard University Press, 2014), 52–53.

35 Anthony Madrid, "The Warrant for Rhyme" (PhD diss., University of Chicago, 2012), 17–18.

36 Kenner, "Rhyme," 385.

37 A. E. Stallings, "Presto Manifesto!" *Poetry* (February 2009), https://www.poetryfoundation.org/poetrymagazine/articles/detail/69202.

38 Simon Jarvis, "Why Rhyme Pleases," *Thinking Verse* 1 (2011), 18.

39 Madrid, "Warrant," 9.

40 *Princeton Encyclopedia*, 1184–85.

41 Kenner, "Rhyme," 384.

42 Madrid, "Warrant," 24.

43 Jarvis, "Why Rhyme Pleases," 41.

44 Much of what follows is excerpted and revised from my essay "Paul Muldoon's Covert Operations," *Modern Philology* 109, no. 2 (November 2011).

45 Steven Matthews, "Muldoon's New Poems and Lyrics," *Poetry Review* 97, no. 1 (Spring 2007): 92.

46 Clair Wills, *Reading Paul Muldoon* (Newcastle upon Tyne: Bloodaxe Books, 1999), 208.

47 See MacDonald P. Jackson, "Shakespeare's Sonnets: Rhyme and Reason in the Dark Lady Series," *Notes and Queries* 244 (1999): 219–22.

48 See John Shoptaw, *On the Outside Looking Out: John Ashbery's Poetry* (Cambridge, MA: Harvard University Press, 1995), on this notion, adapted from Abraham and Török.

49 See Roy Booth, "Standing within the Prospect of Belief: *Macbeth, King James, and Witchcraft*," in John Newton and Jo Bath, eds., *Witchcraft and the Act of 1604* (Leiden, Netherlands: Brill, 2008).

50 Robert Hass, *Twentieth Century Pleasures*, 3rd ed. (New York: Ecco, 2000), 31.

51 Harold Bloom, *The Anxiety of Influence: A Theory of Poetry*, 2nd ed. (New York: Oxford University Press, 1997), 15.

52 Oren Izenberg, *Being Numerous: Poetry and the Ground of Social Life* (Princeton, NJ: Princeton University Press, 2011), 98.

53 *Princeton Encyclopedia*, 1048.

54 W. H. Auden, *The Dyer's Hand* (New York: Vintage International, 1989), 5–6.

55 John Ruskin, *The Genius of John Ruskin: Selections from His Writings*, ed. John D. Rosenberg (Charlottesville, VA: University of Virginia Press, 1998), 137, 170.

56 Richard Brody, *Everything Is Cinema: The Working Life of Jean-Luc Godard* (New York: Metropolitan Books, 2008), 217.

57 Pauline Kael, *I Lost It at the Movies: Film Writings 1954–1965* (New York: Marion Boyars Publishers, 1994), 308.

58 Sullivan, *Pulphead*, 142.

59 Kael, *I Lost It*, 130.

60 James Dickey, *The Selected Poems*, ed. Robert Kirschten (Hanover, NH: Wesleyan University Press, 1998), xv. It is only fair to note that Kirschten is paraphrasing Dickey on Robert Penn Warren.

61 James Dickey, *The Complete Poems of James Dickey*, ed. Ward Briggs (Columbia, SC: University of South Carolina Press, 2013), 859.

62 Joanna Paul, *Film and the Classical Epic Tradition* (Oxford, UK: Oxford University Press, 2013), 38.

63 Quoted in Paul, 39.

64 Paul, 59.

65 Paul, 40.

66 Guy Davenport, *The Geography of the Imagination: Forty Essays* (Boston: David R. Godine, 1997), 42.

67 Michael Herr, *Dispatches* (New York: Vintage International, 1991), 71.

68 Dave Hickey, "The Song in Country Music," in Greil Marcus and Werner Sollors, eds., *A New Literary History of America* (Cambridge, MA: Belknap Press, 2009), 845–46.

69 Christopher Ricks, *Dylan's Visions of Sin* (New York: Ecco, 2003), 14–15.

70 LeRoi Jones (Amiri Baraka), *Blues People: Negro Music in White America* (New York: Harper Perennial, 1999), 50.

71 Ricks, *Dylan's Visions*, 115.

72 Franco 'Bifo' Berardi, *Heroes: Mass Murder and Suicide* (London: Verso, 2015), 220.

73 Stephen Metcalf, "Bob Dylan Is a Genius of Almost Unparalleled Influence, but He Shouldn't Have Gotten the Nobel," *Slate* (October 13, 2016), http://www.slate.com/blogs/browbeat/2016/10/13/why_bob_dylan_shouldn_t_have_gotten_the_nobel_prize_for_literature.html.

74 Willis, *Out of the Vinyl Deeps*, 15.

75 Albert Murray, *Stomping the Blues* (New York: Vintage, 1982), 76.

76 Greil Marcus, "Bob Dylan, Master of Change," *New York Times*, October 13, 2016, http://www.nytimes.com/2016/10/14/opinion/bob-dylan-master-of-change.html.

77 Allen Grossman, *True-Love: Essays on Poetry and Valuing* (Chicago: University of Chicago Press, 2009), 154.

78 Alex Halberstadt, "The Motorcycle Diarist," *New York* (November 25, 2007), http://nymag.com/arts/books/features/24986/.

79 Calvin Bedient, untitled review, *Boston Review* 26, no. 5 (October/November 2001), http://bostonreview.net/BR26.5/bedient.html.

80 George Puttenham, *The Art of English Poesy*, in Gavin Alexander, ed., *Sidney's "The Defense of Poesy" and Selected Renaissance Literary Criticism* (New York: Penguin, 2004), 162.

81 Isobel Armstrong, *Victorian Poetry: Poetry, Poets and Politics* (London: Routledge, 1993), 298, 296.

82 Armstrong, *Victorian Poetry*, 299.

83 Alexander Nehamas, *Nietzsche: Life as Literature* (Cambridge, MA: Harvard University Press, 1987), 127.

84 Friedrich Nietzsche, *Writings from the Late Notebooks*, ed. Rüdiger Bittner (Cambridge, UK: Cambridge University Press, 2003), 39. Hereafter *WL*.

85 Friedrich Nietzsche, *Ecce Homo*, in Aaron Ridley and Judith Norman, eds., *The Anti-Christ, Ecce Homo, Twilight of the Idols, and Other Writings* (New York: Cambridge University Press, 2005), 75.

86 Nietzsche, *WL*, 65.

87 Theodor Adorno, *Aesthetic Theory*, trans. and ed. Robert Hullot-Kentor (Minneapolis: University of Minnesota Press, 1998), 79. (I have slightly altered the translation.)

88 Eve Kosofsky Sedgwick, *Touching Feeling: Affect, Pedagogy, Performativity* (Durham, NC: Duke University Press, 2003), 98.

89 Dante, *The New Life*, trans. Dante Gabriel Rossetti (New York: New York Review Books, 2002), 7.

90 Edward John Trelawny, *Recollections of the Last Days of Shelley and Byron* (London: E. Moxon, 1858), 89.

91 Theodor Adorno et al., *Aesthetics and Politics*, ed. Ronald Taylor (London: Verso, 1980), 189.

92 Sedgwick, *Touching Feeling*, 37.

93 Winfried Menninghaus, *Disgust: The Theory and History of a Strong Sensation*, trans. Howard Eiland and Joel Golb (Albany: State University of New York Press, 2003), 105.

94 See Martha C. Nussbaum, *Hiding from Humanity: Disgust, Shame, and the Law* (Princeton, NJ: Princeton University Press, 2004).

95 Friedrich Nietzsche, *The Portable Nietzsche*, trans. Walter Kaufmann (New York: Penguin, 1968), 42.

96 Nietzsche, *Ecce Homo*, 3.

97 Ezra Pound, *The Cantos of Ezra Pound* (New York: New Directions, 1996), 550.

98 Elizabeth Bishop and Robert Lowell, *Words in Air: The Complete Correspondence Between Elizabeth Bishop and Robert Lowell*, ed.

Thomas Travisano and Saskia Hamilton (New York: Farrar, Straus and Giroux, 2010), 708.

99 Raymond Geuss, *Public Goods, Private Goods* (Princeton, NJ: Princeton University Press, 2001), 27–28.

100 Theodor Adorno, *Lectures on Negative Dialectics*, ed. Rolf Tiedemann (Malden, MA: Polity, 2008), 48; *Minima Moralia: Reflections from Damaged Life*, trans. E. F. N. Jephcott (London: Verso, 1978), 39, 5.

101 Oren Izenberg, "Confiance au Monde; or, the Poetry of Ease," *nonsite* no. 4, December 1, 2011, http://nonsite.org/article/confiance-au-monde-or-the-poetry-of-ease.

102 Theodor Adorno, *Metaphysics: Concept and Problems*, ed. Rolf Tiedemann (Stanford, CA: Stanford University Press, 2000), 110.

103 Grossman, *True-Love*, 154.